The Oakwood

THE
EAST LANCASHIRE
RAILWAY

R. W. RUSH

THE OAKWOOD PRESS
1983

ISBN 0 85361 295 1

AUTHOR'S NOTE

The irregular, elongated T-shaped system which was the East Lancashire Railway formed a valuable alternative route from Liverpool into Yorkshire; alternative that is to the Lancashire & Yorkshire Railway's main line via Manchester. The stem of the T, linking Manchester to this line, was also a useful alternative, though difficult to work owing to its heavy gradients. Continual antagonism between the E.L.R. and the L.&Y.R. was mainly due to a sour grapes attitude on the part of the latter, who were intensely annoyed that the E.L.R. had got in first and taken the prize. How long this antagonism would have lasted is anybody's guess, had it not been brought to a head by the stubborn resistance put up by the little Blackburn Railway, which brought the E.L.R. and L.&Y.R. into an uneasy collaboration to get rid of the small company. From then onwards it was a fairly easy step to continued collaboration and eventual amalgamation of the two rivals.

It was an interesting railway, and probably due to its short independent existence of only thirteen years, it has not received the attention it deserved. This book is an attempt to remedy that lack of attention, though Mr. John Marshall, in his three-volume history of the L.&Y.R., has given it some prominence, and the author wishes to acknowledge his indebtedness to Mr. Marshall for many details. Also the researches of Mr. E. Craven into the locomotive history, and Mr. A. Barlow into engine shed details, must be acknowledged, as these have been very useful in clearing up some obscure points. The track plans of early station layouts have been compiled (not to scale) from old L.M.S.R. track plans, and are designed to show the general layout rather than an accurate detailed map. Locomotive line drawings have been re-drawn from the originals in the author's book on L.&Y.R. locomotives originally published in 1949, and now out of print.

Accrington   ROBERT W. RUSH
January 1983

CONTENTS

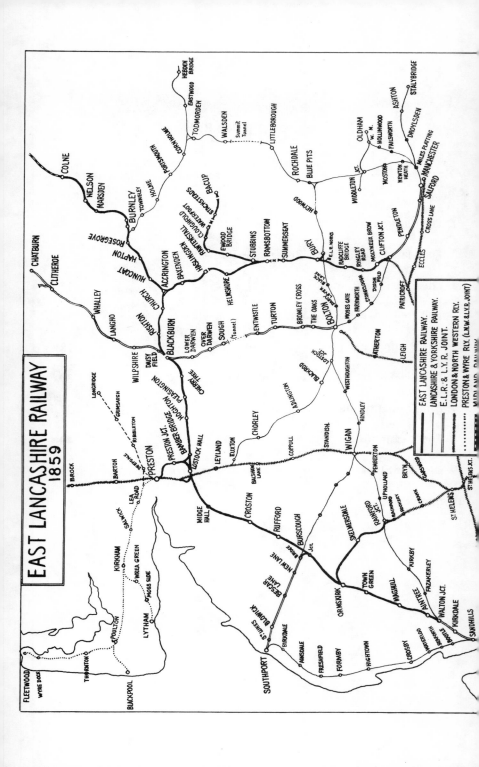

EAST LANCASHIRE RAILWAY 1859

Legend:

EAST LANCASHIRE RAILWAY.
LANCASHIRE & YORKSHIRE RAILWAY.
E.L.R. & L.Y.R. JOINT.
LONDON & NORTH WESTERN RLY.
PRESTON & WYRE RLY. (L.N.W. & L.Y.R. JOINT)
MIDLAND RAILWAY

CHAPTER 1
The Blackburn & Preston Railway

The East Lancashire Railway had an independent existence of only thirteen years, but during that period it seemed to be in a state of perpetual feud with one neighbour or another. It was at loggerheads off and on with its larger neighbour, the Lancashire & Yorkshire Railway, from 1848 until 1857, when there came, at long last, a certain uneasy co-operation, culminating in amalgamation of the two companies in 1859, after much discussion and recrimination. The E.L.R. also crossed swords with the L.N.W.R., the Midland, and the little Blackburn, Darwen & Bolton Railway, which was the only one to score off the E.L.R.

Like most of the larger companies, the E.L.R. was a collection of small concerns which were ultimately welded into one. The unusual feature about the small companies which became the E.L.R. in due course, is that they were all proposed within a few months of each other, and within three years of work commencing on the first of them the whole system was virtually complete and in operation. Even after the amalgamation with the L.&Y.R., the E.L.R. continued to enjoy a certain amount of autonomy; it retained its own offices and executives, its own workshops and its own separate locomotive list. It was not until the coming of J.A.F. Aspinall to the post of Chief Mechanical Engineer of the L.&Y.R. in 1885 that the E.L.R. finally became defunct.

In 1843 a railway was proposed between Blackburn and Preston, with Joseph Locke as its engineer. The Bill for the 12-mile long Blackburn & Preston Railway was passed by Parliament, with no opposition, on 6 June 1844. The route was considerably longer than the turnpike road between the two towns, which was only nine miles, the reason for this being that Preston Corporation objected to a second bridge being built over the River Ribble, there already being one railway bridge which carried the North Union Railway from Wigan. Consequently John Collister, who surveyed the route, as assistant to Locke, planned the line to join the N.U.R. at Farington, 2½ miles south of Preston. Terence Flanagan, who had been for five years an articled pupil of the great Charles Vignoles, and who had been recently elected a member of the Institution of Civil Engineers, was put in charge of the works. Flanagan had a great deal to do with railways in the area, and ultimately became General Manager of the Blackburn, Darwen & Bolton Railway, as will be seen in due course. For construction purposes, the line was divided into two sections, Farington–Hoghton, for which the contractor was John Stephenson, and Hoghton–Blackburn, contracted to Nowell & Hattersley, the two contracts being approximately equal in length. The first sod was cut near

Hoghton Tower on 20 August 1844, and work proceeded satisfactorily. As far as major engineering difficulties were concerned, most of these were in the Hoghton–Blackburn contract; first of all the River Darwen had to be crossed between Hoghton and Pleasington, at a spot known as Hoghton Bottoms, where the river ran through a short but deep gorge. The crossing, by a viaduct of three semicircular 65-foot spans, took eighteen months to complete from the laying of the first stone in December 1844, and the completed structure soared 116 feet above the river. A second crossing of the same river was made near Pleasington, this time by a five-span wooden viaduct 60 feet high. This viaduct sufficed for twenty years, when it was replaced by a stone bridge with an embankment at each end, in 1865. Onwards to the outskirts of Blackburn cuttings and embankments were all that were required, with one crossing of the Leeds & Liverpool Canal, until just before Blackburn station, where the main Bolton Road had to be crossed on the skew. This was achieved by a three-span wooden bridge, later replaced by the present large bowstring girder, supported on stone abutments at each end, and steel columns in the centre. Blackburn station was a commodious two-storey structure "in the Italian style"—which seemed to be descriptive of many public structures in Lancashire—the track level being some 17 feet above the highway, and had an all-over roof in two spans for most of its length.

The western contract was much easier to deal with, being mainly at ground level except for a cutting approaching Hoghton. Two turnpike roads had to be crossed, both by gated level crossings, the main Preston–Wigan road (now the A6) at Bamber Bridge station, and the main street of Hoghton village. The level crossing at Bamber Bridge has been, and still is, a continual source of irritation with its frequent and sometimes lengthy delays to road traffic, but the lie of the land and the numerous buildings have precluded any other method of crossing. There were four intermediate stations on the line, Bamber Bridge, 4 miles from the junction at Farington, Hoghton, 7 miles, Pleasington, 9¼ miles, and Cherry Tree, 10¼ miles. Though there were not much in the way of engineering works, the trend of the line was steadily upwards from near sea level to the foothills of the Pennines at Blackburn, the worst section being 3½ miles at 1 in 100 from Bamber Bridge to beyond Hoghton, then after a short descent to Hoghton Viaduct, the rise continued into Blackburn, mainly at 1 in 200. In spite of this continual upward trend, running time averaged half an hour in each direction. The fares, having been based on the road distance of nine miles, were cheap in comparison with other companies. The completed line was inspected and approved by Col. Coddington on behalf of the Board of Trade, and was opened for passenger traffic on 1 June 1846 though goods traffic was not carried until a further year had elapsed.

There was one small branch line, provided for in the original Act, joining the main line in a trailing junction half a mile before entering

Blackburn station. This was the Blackburn Coal Branch, 528 yards long, and almost entirely on a curve, built to supply coal to two large cotton mills, with several sidings. Though its primary function was lost during the 1930's, the branch still remains in use, serving the main coal depot. Obstructive tactics by the N.U.R. over the access to Preston from Farington soon drove the E.L.R. to find other means of approaching the town. Errington surveyed a route in 1846 for a direct line from Bamber Bridge, with a connection to the Liverpool, Ormskirk & Preston Railway at Lostock Hall. Strong opposition from the N.U.R. and Preston Corporation (who opposed the line for the same reason as before, i.e. a second bridge over the river) was thrown out by Parliament, and the E.L.R. Act was approved on 22 July 1847. The Corporation, however, managed to get some clauses into the Bill, compelling the E.L.R. to build a bridge on the northern bank of the river for a proposed public footway, and enabling the Corporation to lay out the railway embankment with gardens and footpaths—in short, to convert it to a public park. The N.U.R. was to enlarge the station, with an 18-month time limit; if this time were exceeded, the E.L.R. was empowered to complete it. It was to be managed by the N.U.R. but the cost of building and future running costs were to be shared by the two companies, Hawkshaw and Errington being appointed as arbitrators to determine the proportion due from each company. On 28 November 1848 their award was published, but the N.U.R. disagreed, and for eight years the bickering went on until finally settled by no less a person than I.K. Brunel, in 1856, who finally determined that the E.L.R. should pay £25,460 into the joint fund.

On 15 November 1848 the contract for the line was let to McCormick & Daglish. Approaching the River Ribble, which was to be spanned by a bridge of two 25-foot brick arches, and three 100-foot iron spans over the river itself, a large expanse of flat meadowland, liable to flooding, had to crossed. An embankment was proposed here, but the ground was found too soggy to support an embankment, and a viaduct of 52 brick arches, each 30 feet span, was substituted. To support each pier, 17 beech piles, twelve inches square, were sunk to a depth of 20 feet. When the line was ready for opening, it was delayed for almost a year by the collapse of thirteen arches of the viaduct after a severe flood on 25 October 1849. Construction of the remainder of the 2m. 56ch. line from Bamber Bridge posed no difficulties, and the whole, including the extended station, which had a separate frontage in Butler Street, was opened for passenger traffic on 2 September 1850, and for goods on 3 November. In 1913, the East Lancashire side of Preston station was again extended, by two bays and two additional through platforms.

A station on the branch, named Preston Junction, was opened in December 1852, at the fork of the lines going east to Blackburn, and west to Lostock Hall. It was re-erected as an island platform some 200 yards north of its original site in 1885, being renamed Todd Lane seventy years later. In 1866 the viaduct south of the Ribble was in such a parlous state owing to floods and vibration, that it was decided to fill it in and convert it to an embankment. However, the work was shelved, but in 1884 had become imperative. Two years later the embankment was completed, much of the spoil required coming from the site of the new engine shed at Lostock Hall.

CHAPTER 2
The Manchester, Bury & Rossendale Railway

Some thirty miles away, in the southernmost part of the county, a group of Manchester business men got together and proposed a railway from Manchester through Bury and into the Rossendale Valley, following for most of its length the River Irwell. Consequently in October 1843, the Manchester, Bury & Rossendale Railway was formed, with Thomas Gooch and Charles Cawley appointed to survey a possible route. Beginning at Clifton, five miles west of Manchester on the already existing Manchester & Bolton Railway, the line struck off northwards, following the river as nearly as possible, through Radcliffe and Bury, then on to Ramsbottom and Rawtenstall, where it terminated. The route was by no means easy; even by following the river as closely as possible, gradients of 1 in 96 and 1 in 132 were necessary for most of the way to Bury. However, Gooch and Cawley's survey was approved by the directors, and the necessary proceedings were put in motion to obtain Parliamentary sanction for building the line. The Act received the Royal Assent on 4 July 1844. Even while this was going on, the same group of businessmen promoted a second company, the Blackburn, Burnley, Accrington & Colne Extension Railway, which was to leave the M.B.&R. at a point north of Ramsbottom, and proceed via Haslingden to Accrington, where it would fork, the western fork joining the Blackburn & Preston Railway at Blackburn, and the eastern fork going to Burnley and Colne. At the latter place it would make an end-on junction with the Leeds & Bradford Extension Railway (which was already under construction) and so provide an alternative route to Leeds via Accrington, Colne, and Skipton. The B.B.A.&C. Railway was authorised by Act of Parliament on 30 June 1845, with power to lease or sell the undertaking to the M.B.&R. A further Act of 24 July 1845 authorised the amalgamation of the two companies under the title of the East Lancashire Railway. The same Act also allowed the East Lancashire Railway to absorb the Blackburn & Preston Railway. Gooch and Cawley surveyed the Extension Railway, and Sir John Hawkshaw was appointed engineer, but he resigned after three months owing to his commitments to the Manchester & Leeds Railway, Gooch and Cawley being appointed joint engineers in his place. As assistant engineer, John Perring joined the company on 1

December 1845. Running powers were granted in the Act over the Manchester & Bolton Railway from Clifton to Salford, and over the Liverpool & Manchester Railway from Salford into Manchester. These running powers were to be, in the very near future, a considerable cause of friction.

Difficult as the original line to Bury was, the Extension was even worse. Leaving the M.B.&R. route at Stubbins, ¾ mile north of Ramsbottom, it struck off up a side valley and immediately began an unbroken five-mile climb at 1 in 78 through Helmshore and Haslingden (where a short tunnel was required) to a summit at Baxenden, 760 feet above sea level, whence began the 2¼ mile steep drop to Accrington, on gradients of 1 in 71, 47, 38 and 40. From the junction at Accrington both branches were tolerably level, with a ruling gradient to Blackburn of 1 in 122, and to Burnley of 1 in 147. Particularly between Haslingden and Baxenden summit large tracts of sodden peat were encountered, necessitating the tipping of vast quantities of stone in order to form a firm foundation for the track bed, and right down to the line ceasing to function in 1964 this section was always extremely wet. A close watch had to be kept on the two stone overbridges which spanned the track in this section, lest any sign of subsidence occurred.

Beginning at Clifton, the first major constructional item was a 13-arch stone viaduct immediately outside the station, the first crossing of the River Irwell. Next followed 3½ miles of dreary country, partly in cutting and partly on a ledge cut in the hillside, almost continually upward at 1 in 96 to Radcliffe Bridge, the first station. Just before Radcliffe, the Irwell was crossed for the second time by a wooden viaduct of five spans (replaced by an iron one in 1881) and for the third time the river was crossed one mile short of Bury by an iron bridge with a single span of 100 feet. Bury was the principal station on the line, and became the head-quarters of the company, a substantial stone building being erected on the east side of the station to house the offices. A private way from Bolton Street to the offices was commanded by a massive pair of iron gates, each bearing a cast iron shield of the E.L.R. coat of arms. When the station was modernised in 1955, the gates were removed, and one of the shields was cleaned up and painted, then hung up on one wall of the new booking office. The other shield was similarly cleaned up and sent to the Transport Museum in Clapham, London.

Going under Bolton Street in an 80-yard covered way, there was a small goods yard, thence a short cutting, and on a length of more or less ground level track, the Irwell was crossed once more by an iron bridge, and in 2½ miles from Bury the village of Brooksbottom was reached, situated in a loop of the river on a tract of level ground, hemmed in by low hills. The railway formed the chord cutting off this semicircle, and was carried across on a viaduct of eleven stone arches, with a wooden bridge over the river at each end. Plunging through the hill on the northern side of the

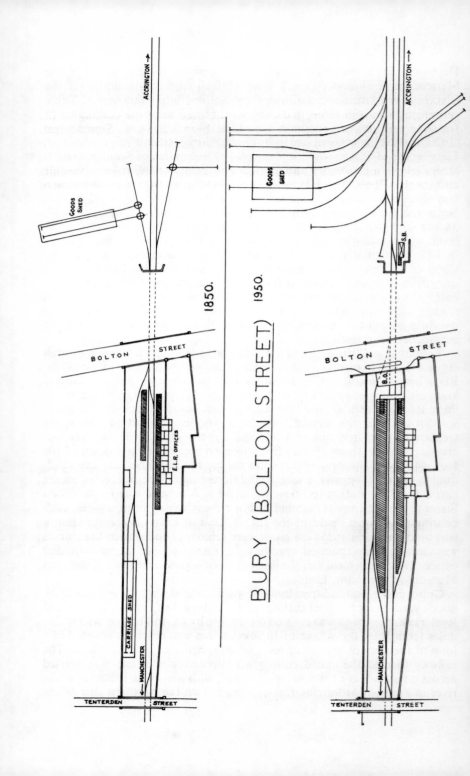

BURY (BOLTON STREET)

1850.

1950.

village by two tunnels—Brooksbottom 423 yards, and Nuttal 115 yards—the line approached Ramsbottom on a long 21-span iron viaduct at a very low level above the river, built on marshy land. There is some confusion regarding Brooksbottom; for most of the time since the coming of the railway the village and its station have been known as Summerseat. Historians disagree as to whether Brooksbottom was the original name or not; to support it there is the name of the tunnel, and also the name of the large cotton mill which stood on the east side of the line, on the opposite side to the village. This was Brooksbottom Mill, and a large proportion of houses in the village were built to house the workpeople of the mill. Be that as it may, the locality has been known for well over a hundred years as Summerseat. The author has an open mind on the subject.

Ramsbottom was a substantial stone-built station, with a level crossing of the Shuttleworth Road immediately north of the platforms, and a fair sized goods yard. Three-quarters of a mile farther north, at the extreme end of the goods yard, was the junction between the original M.B.&R. line and the Extension Railway, at Stubbins, which had a station on the Rawtenstall line only, the Accrington Extension passing immediately behind the station. Taking the Rawtenstall line first, this ran along the valley floor for 3½ miles to Rawtenstall, mostly on a rising grade of 1 in 132, crossing the Irwell at Alderbottom (¼ mile from Stubbins) by a two-span wooden viaduct, and, after crossing the meandering river twice more, passed through Ewood Bridge station. From here, until the opening of the Extension line, a horse bus service was provided to Haslingden. A twelfth crossing of the Irwell brought the line to its terminus. After inspection by General Pasley for the B.O.T., on 23 September 1846, the line throughout from Clifton to Rawtenstall was opened two days later amid great celebrations. The first train left Manchester Victoria at 12.35 p.m., consisting of 18 carriages and two locomotives, and after a normal run of 35 minutes to Bury a stop was made while a further 15 carriages were attached, and some local bigwigs taken on board. The rest of the run to Rawtenstall was achieved in a further half hour. The public service began on 28 September, with 14 trains between Manchester and Bury, plus an additional five trains through to Rawtenstall. In 1847 a new station was opened at Ringley Road, 2½ miles from Clifton, and in 1853 another at Molyneux Brow, 1 mile from the junction.

On 13 October 1845 the contract for the Extension Railway from Stubbins to Accrington was let to John Brogden, and work commenced at once. The remainder of the line, between Blackburn and Colne, was divided into two almost equal parts, the first from Blackburn to Hapton being given to William Hattersley, and the second, from Hapton to Colne, to a consortium, Brogden, Smith & Pearce. To supervise the whole works Joseph Locke and John Errington were appointed engineers to the whole company in January 1847. Cawley resigned on 28 May 1846, and

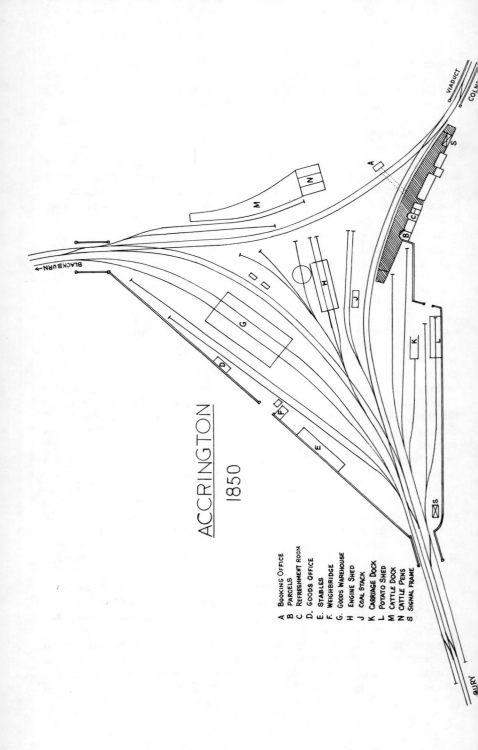

ACCRINGTON
1850

A BOOKING OFFICE
B PARCELS
C REFRESHMENT ROOM
D. GOODS OFFICE
E. STABLES
F. WEIGHBRIDGE
G. GOODS WAREHOUSE
H ENGINE SHED
J COAL STACK
K CARRIAGE DOCK
L POTATO SHED
M CATTLE DOCK
N CATTLE PENS
S SIGNAL FRAME

BLACKBURN →

VIADUCT
COLN

BURY

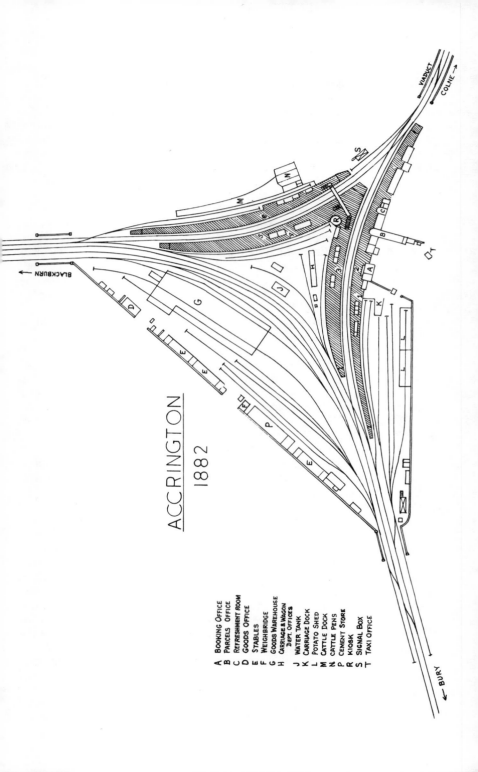

ACCRINGTON
1882

A BOOKING OFFICE
B PARCELS OFFICE
C REFRESHMENT ROOM
D GOODS OFFICE
E STABLES
F WEIGHBRIDGE
G GOODS WAREHOUSE
H CARRIAGE & WAGON
   DEPT. OFFICES
J WATER TANK
K CARRIAGE DOCK
L POTATO SHED
M CATTLE DOCK
N CATTLE PENS
P CEMENT STORE
R KIOSK
S SIGNAL BOX
T TAXI OFFICE

BLACKBURN

VIADUCT

COLNE

BURY

his place as resident engineer was taken by John Perring.

The Alpine nature of the Stubbins–Accrington line necessitated a considerable amount of heavy constructional work. Leaving Stubbins, the Irwell was crossed at Alderbottom by a six-span timber viaduct a few yards downstream from that on the Rawtenstall route, both viaducts being replaced in 1881 by steel girder bridges. The Extension now left the Irwell valley, and clawed its way up a side valley, rising continuously at 1 in 78 for five miles, cut through some hilly country, and crossing two other ravines by a nine-arch stone viaduct at Lumb, and the three-span Ogden viaduct. Leaving Helmshore station there was an eleven-arch stone viaduct on a curve. At Helmshore station, 2½ miles from Stubbins, the old Blackburn–Bury road was crossed on the level (the only level crossing on the Accrington line) which right down to the demise of the railway was to be the cause of much delay and frustration to road traffic. Though various schemes were proposed from time to time to replace the crossing by a bridge, none of them came to anything due to the awkward geographical position; it was found impracticable to provide either an overbridge or an underpass at the site. Still climbing at 1 in 78, after crossing Grane Road on a tubular iron bridge of Fairbairn's pattern, and cutting through a small hill by Haslingden Tunnel (146 yards), Haslingden station was reached, two miles from Helmshore, and the final one-mile length to Baxenden summit began, most of this being in cutting through sodden peat, which caused no end of trouble, as has been mentioned earlier. Baxenden summit was the highest point reached by the E.L.R. until 1852, when Bacup—on the extension from Rawtenstall —took the title at 801 feet. The 2¼ mile descent from the summit to Accrington was somewhat hair-raising, since more than 75% of it was on reverse curves, and the ruling gradient of 1 in 38 was steep. At Accrington South Junction the line forked, westward to Blackburn, and eastward to Colne; a direct line was put in here, from west junction to east junction, to allow of through running from Blackburn to Colne.

In spite of the importance of the junctions here, the station provided at Accrington was one of the most inconvenient and illogical structures imaginable. It consisted of a short, low platform 60 yards long, with two solid stone buildings which housed the waiting rooms and the usual offices. On the centre of the roof of the easterly building was a short clock tower, showing four faces (this was removed when the station was rebuilt in 1882). The station was situated at the East Junction, and on the up line to Bury; no other platforms were provided. To make matters worse, the booking office was a separate building away across four tracks on the down Colne side, at the summit of a steep path leading up the side of the embankment from the Blackburn road. In later years a ticket platform was put in at South Junction, but this was for staff purposes only, and passengers were not allowed to use it.

The working of this monstrous aberration was a masterpiece of ingenuity, worked out by James Smithells, the Traffic Manager of the

E.L.R. Like most things, though good in theory, it fell down badly in practice. Trains were timed so as to arrive from all three directions simultaneously, and as each train had one or more through carriages for the other two directions, there was a veritable orgy of shunting, each train having to visit the solitary platform in turn. Fifteen minutes were allowed for the "circus" at Accrington, but rarely, if ever, was this adhered to. The E.L.R. did not have much of a reputation for punctuality, though it was better than the L.&Y.R.—which was not saying much—so trains did NOT arrive simultaneously, and the exchange of coaches was often prolonged over half an hour or more. The astonishing thing is that this state of affairs was tolerated for 34 years, as it was not until 1882 that an entirely new Y-shaped station, with six platforms, was built under the direction of Sturges Meek, the L.&Y.R. engineer, and the "circus" disappeared for good. The goods station was situated on the west side of the triangle, and remained there until demolished in 1971. In the centre of the triangle was a small engine shed.

The western branch posed some difficulties, with the 434-yard tunnel immediately after leaving Blackburn station, and a viaduct of 18 timber spans, each of 12 feet, resting on wooden piles, which crossed the Rishton reservoir belonging to the Leeds & Liverpool Canal Company. This was made into an embankment some forty years later. The general trend was upward from Blackburn for the whole 5¼ miles to Accrington, but at no part was the grade steeper than 1 in 122. Rishton station, 2¾ miles from Blackburn, was a substantial stone affair combining the offices, stationmaster's house and goods shed all in the same building. Thence to Church & Oswaldtwistle, 1½ miles, the Aspen Valley had to be crossed by means of a wooden viaduct of 33 spans, 25 feet each, built for single line only, and 70 feet high at its maximum. For many years there was a speed restriction of 25 m.p.h. over this structure, which was gradually turned into a double-line embankment, authorised by a general purposes Act obtained in 1889. On 20 March 1891 the first load of ashes was tipped, and filling continued until 1925, when the embankment was completed and the speed restriction lifted. Crossing the main Accrington–Blackburn road by an iron bridge, the line then ran onto Church viaduct, seven 40-foot span brick arches, and into Church station—which was then 300 yards nearer Accrington than its present site. Onwards into Accrington the line was dead straight and about 15 feet above ground level on a low embankment. The line was inspected by Capt. Wynne and passed for traffic on 17 June 1848, the official opening being two days later. The Blackburn & Preston Railway having been amalgamated with the E.L.R. by the Act of 21 July 1845, trains began running through between Preston and Accrington.

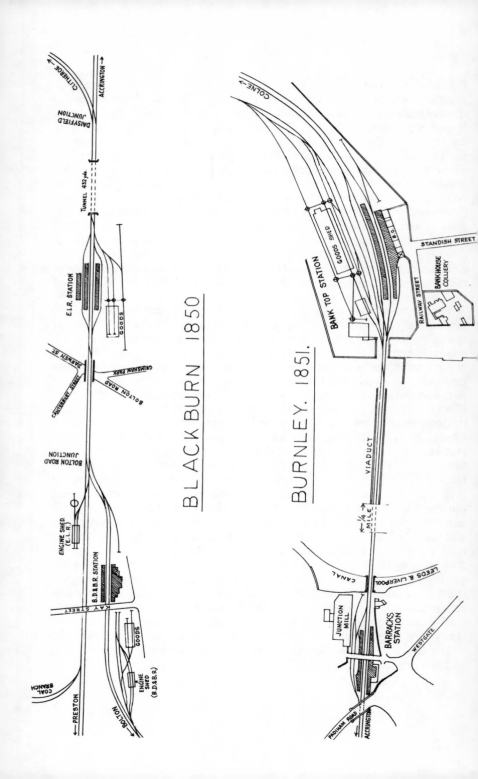

BLACKBURN 1850

BURNLEY. 1851.

CHAPTER 3
The Extension Railway

The Extension Railway was still not complete, being officially approved after inspection by Capt. Simmons on 15 August 1848. One month later, on 18 September, the section north-eastwards from Accrington to Burnley (Barracks) was opened, a length of 5½ miles. This began with the Accrington viaduct, which adjoined the platform end, and consisted of 40-foot brick spans, 21 in all, faced with stone, and had a maximum height of 60 feet. The whole structure was built on a continuous curve of 40 chains radius. Four piers, two at each side of the bed of the River Hyndburn, began to subside before construction was complete, and had to be taken down and rebuilt. The viaduct continued to give trouble, and on 4 July 1866, the engineer of the L.&Y.R., Sturges Meek, closed it completely and for fifteen months until reconstruction work was finished on 11 September 1867 trains were terminated at Accrington and Huncoat (the first station to the east) and a service of horse vehicles substituted. From the eastern end of the viaduct the line ran in cutting for 500 yards through rising ground until it came out again at ground level alongside the municipal cemetery, and a short length of low embankment ensued to Huncoat station, which had a brickworks on the south side and a colliery on the north. A siding led off into the colliery, but there was no rail connection with the brickworks. Entering Huncoat station a minor road through the village was crossed by a gated crossing, which in later days boasted the second largest and heaviest gates on the L.&Y.R. system, necessitated by the crossing being at an acute angle, and including the colliery access. The trend having been steadily upward from Blackburn, at the cemetery the conditions were reversed, the line falling to the valley of the Lancashire Calder at Burnley. On this section there were no major works, though the Leeds & Liverpool canal was crossed twice within 150 yards approaching Rosegrove, 4¾ miles from Accrington. For the time being, the line ended at Burnley (Barracks) station, ¾ mile further on, until the Calder viaduct of 15 stone spans was completed between Barracks and Bank Top stations. The final 5½ miles on to Colne was again with an upward trend, mainly at 1 in 144, and contained two further viaducts, one of five brick spans at Marsden, and the other of six stone arches adjoining Colne station. Here there was an end-on junction with the Midland Railway, who built the station, this and the goods yard being made joint property of both companies. The section from Burnley Barracks to Colne was opened for public service on 1 February 1849.

On 12 March 1849 occurred what has gone down in railway annals as the "Battle of Clifton Junction". E.L.R. trains from Bury and beyond had to travel over L.&Y.R. metals from Clifton Junction to Salford, for which the L.&Y.R. exacted toll according to the number of passengers.

This was agreed by the two parties, and worked easily enough as far as stopping trains were concerned, for tickets could be checked by L.&Y.R. officials at Clifton. The trouble began when the E.L.R. decided to put on some expresses, and the L.&Y.R. demanded that these should stop at Clifton to collect tickets. To this the E.L.R. refused to agree, saying that they had nothing to hide, and their ticket ledgers were open to inspection by the L.&Y.R. at any time. Being devious themselves at that period, the L.&Y.R. officials could not believe the E.L.R. were not perpetrating a swindle, and declared war on the officials at Bury. When the first express train arrived at Clifton about 10.30 a.m. on this particular day, the driver was compelled to stop, since a gang of L.&Y.R. platelayers had placed a great baulk of timber across the track and had chained it to the rails. On the train coming to a halt, an L.&Y.R. official demanded tickets, but was told by the guard that there weren't any, as, according to regulations, they had been collected at Radcliffe. Having got wind of possible trouble, the E.L.R. had requested the help of the police, and a large detachment of officers from Bury and Pendleton were present at the scene. The L.&Y.R. then moved up an empty passenger train on the same line with the object of taking off the E.L.R. passengers and conveying them to Salford. Meanwhile a party of E.L.R. men moved in and lifted away the timber obstruction, rather strangely without any opposition from the L.&Y.R., possibly because of the presence of the police. The E.L.R. train now moved up to touch buffers with the L.&Y.R. train, and there ensued a "push-of-war" between the two, with neither making any progress. The L.&Y.R. brought up another engine to help in the proceedings, and the E.L.R. retaliated by moving a heavy train loaded with stone on to the L.&Y.R. down line. By midday the contest had reached its climax, with no less than eight trains cluttering up the junction, and producing a complete impasse. Perhaps seeing no way out of this mess, all the L.&Y.R. officials quietly melted away, leaving the field in charge of Henry Blackmore, the L.&Y.R. passenger superintendent. Having been left to face the irate passengers alone, and no doubt seeing the futility of the proceedings, he ordered the L.&Y.R. trains away, and the gangers to disperse. After the chaos had sorted itself out, the beleaguered E.L.R. express went on its way, some two hours late, treating the locals to triumphant "crows" from its whistle all the way into Salford. As a result of this, and further pinpricks from the L.&Y.R., the Bury company proposed its own independent route into Manchester, via Whitefield and Cheetham Hill. A Bill was prepared, but seeing the red light, the L.&Y.R. came to terms, and the line between Clifton Junction and Manchester Victoria was vested jointly in the two companies, under the title of the Clifton & Manchester Railway.

One of the worst accidents on the L.&Y.R. system occurred on the East Lancashire Division (as it had then become) on 3 September 1860. Three heavy excursion trains were returning from Manchester to Burnley and

Colne, operating under time interval. Climbing the long bank from Ramsbottom to Baxenden summit, the first train got through uneventfully, but when the second train was passing Grane Road bridge, twelve carriages broke away from the rear and commenced running backwards down the incline. Near Helmshore station, the runaways crashed into the engine of the third train. The engine was thrown on its side, and the first three carriages damaged, but fortunately the couplings held, and the rest of the train, though partially derailed, remained upright and in line. The runaway coaches, however, were badly smashed, eleven passengers being killed and 62 injured in various degrees.

A branch which was not E.L.R. property, but nevertheless concerned that company considerably, was built by the L.&Y.R. It began at Todmorden, in a triangular junction with the Manchester & Leeds line, and was built up the valley of the Yorkshire Calder, and over the watershed at Copy Pit summit, into the valley of the Lancashire Calder, the headwaters of the two rivers being only a very short distance apart, though flowing in opposite directions. The line, known as the Burnley Branch, was proposed in 1844, and authorised by the Manchester & Leeds Railway Act of 30 June 1845. Planned as a single line nine miles in length, the contract was let to Faviell in the following October for £140,000. Later in the same month it was decided to build it as a double line, and this Faviell agreed to do for a further £66,000. In September 1847 the newly-formed L.&Y.R. was experiencing financial difficulties, work on the line was ordered to be stopped, and was not resumed until the following May, with orders to reduce it to single line again, but with earthworks wide enough for double track. Work after this was haphazard, and in June 1849 Faviell was relieved of his contract, and the construction completed by direct labour. The single line was finished by October 1849, and was opened on 12 November. There was a steep climb from both ends, the ruling gradient being 1 in 65 from the Yorkshire side and 1 in 68 from the Lancashire end, Copy Pit summit being at 762 feet above sea level. There were four tunnels, and Burnley (Thorneyholme) station was reached in 8¾ miles from Todmorden. A further half mile led to a junction with the E.L.R. Accrington–Burnley line at Gannow Junction, just outside Rosegrove, though this was the subject of a separate contract, and was not opened until August 1850. At this date began an alternative through route from East Lancashire into Yorkshire, which, although difficult to work, became a very valuable one. It was not doubled until 1857. Though not part of the E.L.R. it was made an appendage of the East Lancashire Division of the L.&Y.R. after the amalgamation. The passenger service over this line ceased in November 1965, after being under threat for several years, but it continues to carry considerable goods traffic, and is in use during the summer months for excursion trains.

A bad accident occurred at Burnley (Thorneyholme) station on 13 July 1852, due entirely to bad working practices, a thing the L.&Y.R. was noted for at that period. Two enormous excursion trains had been sent off, loaded with schoolchildren, one of 45 carriages to York, and the other of 35 carriages to Goole. Owing to their length, they were loaded and despatched from the E.L.R.'s sidings at Gannow Junction, and they were intended to be dealt with in the same way on their return. The old Thorneyholme station at that date had only one platform, a dead end, and with a capacity of only six carriages, placed on a siding off the through lines to Gannow Junction. A weighted point lever, which normally lay over to open the platform line, was the only control. On the return of the excursions, late at night, it was intended to stop the train short of the platform points, uncouple the engines (both trains were double-headed) and run them off to the locomotive sidings, then allow the carriages to run down to Gannow sidings by gravity. The first train, from York, was dealt with safely in this manner, but with the Goole train things went sadly wrong. To begin with, the station was badly understaffed; there were only a porter (named Parker) and a night watchman (Grant) on duty, so Parker persuaded two of his pals, neither of them connected with the railway, to come and help. When the Goole train arrived, Parker told one of his friends (Crabtree) to hold over the platform points, thus keeping the line open to Gannow sidings. However, Crabtree thought he ought to go and help Grant, who was collecting tickets, so he called to the second man, Bridge, "Here, Tom, come and hold these points". Bridge did so, but no sooner had he taken hold of the lever than the driver of one of the engines called to him to shift the points leading to the engine shed. Bridge went over to the shed points, and of course released the weighted lever, which immediately set the points for the dead-end platform road. The guard released the brakes on the standing train, which began to run down the line, and, diverted by the platform points, crashed into the buffer stops. Though only moving slowly, the great weight of the train caused havoc among the coaches, and three children and one teacher were killed, more than 100 being injured. The Board of Trade inspector made some extremely scathing comments concerning the recruiting of amateurs to station work, and severely censured the L.&Y.R. for its parsimony in not employing an adequate staff. He also pointed out that the damage and casualties would have been much less if some of the carriage buffers had not over-ridden the others, and recommended that all buffers should be at a standard height. This accident was one (among many) which led the B.O.T. in 1858 to insist that all points should be worked by levers fixed in one group and under the control of one man. Thus the signal box was born.

Thorneyholme station was replaced in 1866 by a new through station on the Gannow line, and on the opposite side of the main road from the old station, being known henceforth as Burnley (Manchester Road).

CHAPTER 4
To Liverpool and Southport

A fourth company was brought into being on 24 August 1844, when it was proposed to build a line from Preston to Liverpool via Ormskirk, with a branch from the last-named to Southport. The Bill was opposed strongly by the North Union and Liverpool & Manchester Railways, since it would shorten the distance between Preston and Liverpool by some ten miles, compared with their existing route by Wigan and Parkside Junction. The Southport branch was also opposed by the Liverpool, Crosby & Southport and Manchester & Southport Railways, neither of which had even received their own Parliamentary authorisation at the time. The Liverpool, Ormskirk & Preston Railway Bill would have been thrown out by the House of Lords had not the promotors agreed to withdraw the Southport branch; the Bill then passed all its final stages and received the Royal Assent on 16 August 1846.

The line began at a junction with the N.U.R. at Penwortham, two miles south of Preston, and proceeded via Rufford, Ormskirk, and Aintree to a junction with the Liverpool & Bury Railway (a protégé of the L.&Y.R.) at Walton Junction. From here to Liverpool, and the Liverpool terminus itself, were, by the terms of the Act, to be made the joint property of both companies. The L.O.&P. were required to pay to the L.&B. half the cost of works already under construction on the joint line. Other clauses in the Act provided for a short branch from Ormskirk to Skelmersdale, the North Mersey branch to the Liverpool docks, and a direct connecting line from Penwortham to join the Blackburn & Preston Railway at Lostock Hall. With the approval of three-fifths of the shareholders, the Act allowed the sale or lease of the whole line to the E.L.R., and after the usual negotiations, the amalgamation took place on 17 October 1846. As engineers to the E.L.R., Locke and Errington took charge of the works, and Sturges Meek was appointed resident engineer for the Liverpool area. McKenzie, Brassey & Stephenson were awarded the contract, their tender of £200,698 was accepted, with completion date 1 July 1848. There was a penalty clause of £300 per week for time in excess of this date. Work began with the cutting of the first sod at Maghull on 16 March 1847. The total distance between Liverpool and Preston was 29¾ miles, of which 3½ miles at the Liverpool end was joint property, and two miles from Penwortham to Preston running powers over the N.U.R. As was very common in the middle 1840's, construction time was hopelessly underestimated, and no allowance had been made for unforeseen difficulties, of which the worst were encountering masses of wet peat in the Douglas valley at Rufford, and a smaller morass at Croston. Funds began to run out, and at the end of September 1847 orders were given to keep expenditure down to a minimum, yet within a few months the contractors were being urged to take on more men in order to speed up construction. The penalty clause in the contract was waived in January 1848.

The embankment at Rufford was a continual headache. All material tipped to make it simply disappeared into the bog overnight, and only by constructing a 400-yard timber framework supported on wooden piles driven 40 feet into the ground was a firm foundation obtained. The River Douglas itself was crossed by a wooden viaduct. At Croston the same method had to be used, but in this case the peat bog was much smaller. Since the whole of the line passed through the south-western part of the county, which was more or less flat, with only low hills around Ormskirk, there were no other heavy engineering works to be undertaken. Nevertheless, the approach to Ormskirk involved a ruling gradient of 1 in 132 from the Liverpool end and 1 in 142 from the northern side, roughly five miles in each direction. North of Rufford there was nothing steeper than 1 in 204. Owing to opposition from the N.U.R., the direct junction at Penwortham was not constructed, and when trains did begin running they had to reverse at Lostock Hall. This state of affairs lasted until November 1850, when the E.L.R. Preston Extension was opened, enabling direct running into Preston via Preston Junction. Even so, this was a rather circuitous route for Liverpool trains, and eventually in 1891 the L.&Y.R. constructed the Farington Curve, which was for all practical purposes the original junction at Penwortham, proposed in the L.O.&P.R. Act, cutting the overall distance by 2½ miles. The whole line from Walton to Preston was completed by the end of March 1849, and was officially opened on 2 April.

The opening of the L.O.&P.R. line led immediately to another feud over the fares between Liverpool and Preston. The E.L.R. route being considerably shorter than that of the N.U.R. and L.N.W.R. via Wigan, the latter feared a loss of traffic to the new line. The E.L.R. fixed its fares at 5/- (25p.) first class, 3/9 (18½p.) second class, and 2/6 (12½p.) third class, whereupon the L.N.W.R. faction promptly brought theirs down to 4/- (20p.), 3/- (15p.) and 2/- (10p.). In response to this the E.L.R. came down to the same fares, and two days later the rivals reduced theirs to the knock-down prices of 1/- (5p.), 9d. (3½p.) and 6d. (2½p.). Realising they had gone too far, the L.N.W.R. raised their fares on the following day to 3/6 (17½p.), 2/6 (12½p.) and 2/- (10p.), whereupon the E.L.R. brought in 2/- (10p.), 1/6 (7½p.) and 1/- (5p.). How long this would have gone on is anybody's guess, but at last someone in authority produced some common sense, and a meeting of both parties settled the issue with both charging the same, 5/- (25p.), 3/9 (18½p.) and 2/6 (12½p.).

Meanwhile at the Liverpool end a start had been made on the jointly owned section from Walton Junction into the terminus, in Tithebarn Street, Liverpool. Hawkshaw, as engineer to the L.&Y.R., was put in charge of the works, and appointed as his assistant William Dodds, who, when the works were finished, became locomotive superintendent for the

Liverpool District, a post he held until his retirement in 1891. Though the order to begin work was given on 23 July 1847, no progress was made for over a year, and the E.L.R., far from satisfied with the planned works, was even considering building a station of their own. However, as they were committed to a half share in the cost of the joint section, eventually they dropped their idea of independence. George Thomson's tender of £48,000 was accepted, with a guarantee from him of completion in six months. Work began on 4 June 1849 and was completed by 8 November of the same year. Involved in the works was the demolition of 540 slum dwellings, and a Presbyterian chapel 140 years old, which had to be rebuilt on a different site at the railways' expense. The building of the line was no easy task, since the bulk of it was above ground level, and several bridges of one kind or another were required, first to cross the Leeds & Liverpool Canal basin, for which four lattice girder spans were required, one of 120 feet, one of 112 feet, and two of 70 feet. The final stage into Tithebarn Street was on a continuous series of arches, the track bed rising at 1 in 84 and 1 in 94 to the terminus, which was 25 feet above street level, this being necessary in order to avoid closing several streets below the station premises.

Tithebarn Street station was an imposing structure, rising to 90 feet above street level with its two storeys, with a main façade of 117 feet, and two single-storey wings at right angles 193 feet long. Separate booking offices, refreshment rooms, waiting rooms, etc., were provided for each company, the L.&Y.R taking possession of the western side of the station, leaving the E.L.R. with the eastern wing. As built, the station contained five platforms, a single arrival platform on the extreme eastern side, and two pairs of departure platforms. The E.L.R. was not happy with these arrangements, since it meant that arriving L.&Y.R. trains, after disgorging their passengers, then had to shunt across both E.L.R. platforms to get to their own departure side, causing delays to E.L.R. trains. Though the E.L.R. protested about these manoeuvres, the L.&Y.R. took no notice. When the station opened on 11 March 1850, the L.&Y.R. was in complete possession of the western side. In the following August the E.L.R. applied to the Railway Commissioners for a ruling on the dispute, but no record has been found of their reply, which was given on 13 January 1851. It would seem, however, that the Commissioners ruled in favour of the L.&Y.R, since no alteration was made.

The platforms were covered by two iron and glass roofs, one of which was 638 feet long, and tapering from 135 feet to 128 feet wide, in one span, without central supports. The other roof, on the E.L.R. side, was only 161 feet long, with a span of 78 feet. It says much for the work force that the whole station was completed within six months of the finishing of the arches on which it was supported.

Included in the plans for the extension into Tithebarn Street was the construction of a jointly-owned branch from Kirkdale to the North

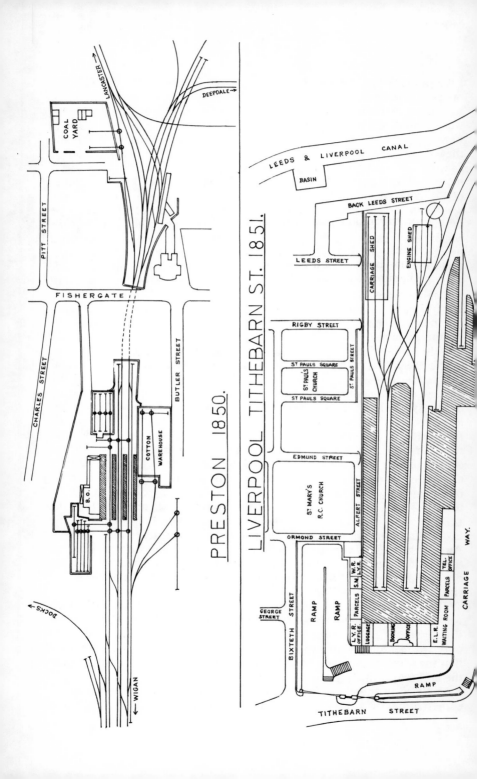

PRESTON 1850.

LIVERPOOL TITHEBARN ST. 1851.

Docks, which had been authorised in the original L.O.&P.R. Act to that company alone. However, by the Manchester & Leeds Act of 1847 (which authorised the formation of the L.&Y.R) the latter was empowered to take a half share in the North Docks branch, not without some opposition from the E.L.R., on payment to the latter company half the cost of the works completed so far. On 7 June 1848 the E.L.R. gave notice that they intended to proceed with the branch, and had purchased some of the land, on which the L.&Y.R. paid £10,260 to the E.L.R. under the terms of the Act. Sturges Meek drew up the plans, and a contract was produced with a contractor named McCormick for the building of the line, but eight months later the contract still had not been signed. On 12 February 1849 construction was postponed indefinitely, probably through lack of capital, and nothing further had been done when the powers expired on 1 August 1853. Having sunk a considerable amount of capital into the branch, the L.&Y.R. then applied for powers to take over the works, authorised by an Act dated 2 June 1854; the branch, substantially as before, now also had separate connections to Stanley, Wellington, Nelson, and Sandon Docks. By one clause the E.L.R. was allowed to become a joint owner of all the lines on notice being given before 1 September 1855, thereupon becoming liable to the L.&Y.R for half the cost. However, should the E.L.R. refuse joint ownership, the L.&Y.R. was compelled to pay the E.L.R. £98,861. These arrangements would have restored the status quo of the original Act, but in the event the E.L.R. chose not to accept joint ownership, and duly received payment from the L.&Y.R., who then proceeded alone with the works. George Thomson's tender of £41,000 was accepted, and construction began immediately, the works being completed on 26 March 1855.

The L.O.&P.R. was now complete except for the Skelmersdale branch, and the connection from Burscough to Southport. Work on the branch from Ormskirk had been suspended in 1848, and had not been revived. Nevertheless, an Act was obtained on 4 August 1853 authorising the extension of the branch from Skelmersdale to a junction with the St. Helens Railway at Rainford. Work on the whole branch then commenced on 25 May 1857 under contract with Thomas Stone for £15,317. Material dug out from the cutting at Ormskirk was transported to Rufford, on the Preston line, to convert the timber viaduct over the River Douglas to an embankment. The St. Helens Railway was opened to Rainford Junction, on the Liverpool—Bury line, on 1 February 1858, and an extension to join the E.L.R. branch was built, avoiding Rainford Junction and passing over the Liverpool—Bury line. At the same time a curve from north to east was built (without parliamentary sanction) to allow the E.L.R. access to Rainford Junction. Col. Yolland inspected the E.L.R. works on 22 February 1858, and they were opened to traffic on 1 March. A joint service of trains was operated with the St. Helens Railway between Ormskirk, Rainford, St. Helens and Widnes. After the amalgamation of the St. Helens Railway with the L.N.W.R. on 29 July 1864, the E.L.R. (then part of the L.&Y.R) was granted running powers from Rainford to St. Helens, but not to Widnes. The Southport connection was the cause of considerable trouble. On 22 April 1847 an Act was passed authorising the Manchester & Southport Railway (of which the L.&Y.R was a considerable shareholder) to build a line from Pendlebury, on the Manchester & Bolton line, via Wigan and Burscough to Southport, with connections to the L.O.&P.R. at Burscough, and to collieries in the Wigan area. Almost the first work undertaken by the new company was to construct a bridge through the L.O.&P.R. embankment at Burscough, since the L.O.&P.R. works were well advanced. With the completion of the section from Pendlebury to Wigan, the L.&Y.R. vetoed further construction, since they were in financial trouble. Matters remained in abeyance until 1852, when the local bigwigs in Southport having exerted considered pressure, Hawkshaw was asked to re-estimate the cost of the remaining 17 miles from Wigan, which he put at £120,000. No futher action was taken, however, and the people of Southport applied to the Court of the Queen's Bench for a *mandamus* compelling the construction of the railway. This was granted in August 1852, and, faced with the necessity of going ahead with the works, the L.&Y.R. sought to reduce the cost by building the railway as a single line, which only saved £16,000. On 24 February 1853 the contract was let to Thomas Davies, recommended by no less a person than I.K. Brunel.

As a means of shedding more of the cost, the L.&Y.R. accepted a suggestion from the E.L.R. that the Burscough–Southport section should be built jointly, with the west–south connection at Burscough from the E.L.R. to the M.&S.R. to be built by the E.L.R. alone—thus giving the latter a direct connection between Liverpool and Southport, which had hitherto been denied to them by the terms of the original L.O.&P.R. Act of 1846. Another Act was obtained by the E.L.R. on 3 July 1854 authorising the joint line, with the curve at Burscough, and a separate approach line and terminus in Southport. These last were the result of opposition from the Liverpool, Crosby & Southport Railway, who refused to let the E.L.R. use their station in Southport, though they were quite willing to let the L.&Y.R. use it.

There were no major engineering works on the whole line from Wigan, apart from bridges over the Douglas and the canal, and two short cuttings on the Wigan–Burscough section. The single line was ready for opening early in 1855, but the certificate was withheld by the B.O.T. until the joint section had been doubled. On completion of this work, Capt. Tyler inspected the line again on 4 April 1855, and the line was opened forthwith. Stations on the joint section were Burscough Bridge, 9¾ miles from Wigan, New Lane 11 miles, Bescar Lane 13 miles, and Southport 17 miles. The distinction of being the lowest station on the whole L.&.Y.R.

system was held by Bescar Lane, which was only 12½ feet above sea level. The E.L.R. station in Southport was in London Street, very close to the L.C.&S.R. station in Chapel Street. About 1860 (the date cannot be confirmed) E.L.R. services were transferred to Chapel Street, and London Street became a goods depot. In the present century London Street again became a passenger station, with the construction of several platforms for excursion traffic, and was then virtually an extension of Chapel Street. Additional stations were opened at St. Luke's (Southport) in 1883, and Blowick, 1½ miles from Chapel Street, in 1871.

Another battle of cheap fares began with the opening of the joint line to Southport, for with the curve at Burscough the E.L.R. obtained a competitive route between Liverpool and Southport, although 4½ miles longer than the L.C.&S.R. line via Formby. The battle went on until fares had reached the ridiculous level of 6d. (2½p.) single and 9d. (3½p.) return, for the whole distance, and was not resolved until March 1856, when fares by either route were fixed at 1/6 (7½p.) single, and 2/6 (12½p.) return. At one stage the E.L.R. was offering a 2/6 (12½p.) return fare between Manchester and Southport via Bury, Accrington, Preston and Burscough, a most circuitous route which few passengers took advantage of.

CHAPTER 5
The Bacup Branch

The original line of the Manchester, Bury & Rossendale Railway had ended at Rawtenstall, but there was still a length of 4½ miles to Bacup, at the head of the Irwell Valley, a town of comparable size to Rawtenstall. Bacup was situated at the extreme end of the valley, with hills on three sides, the only easy way out being by the road to Rawtenstall. In all three other directions, to Todmorden, Burnley, or Rochdale, a stiff climb was necessary. A railway did eventually arrive at Bacup from Rochdale, but it was not until 1881, and then only after clawing its way over a 962-foot summit.

From Rawtenstall the route surveyed was subject to a ruling gradient of 1 in 72, almost half the distance being at this inclination, and rising all the way to Bacup. On 18 January 1847 the contract for the extension was given to Birtram, Parker, Swindell & Horner, with a time limit of 10½ months. Work began on the ascent of the narrow valley, and for the first two miles to Waterfoot the going was fairly easy, the track being laid as close to the river as possible; the single line was opened to a station in the village on 27 March 1847, though the station was actually named Newchurch, after a somewhat larger adjoining village. Beyond Waterfoot was a tortuous deep rocky defile known locally as "The Glen", so narrow that the roadway through it, closely following the river, had to be built on

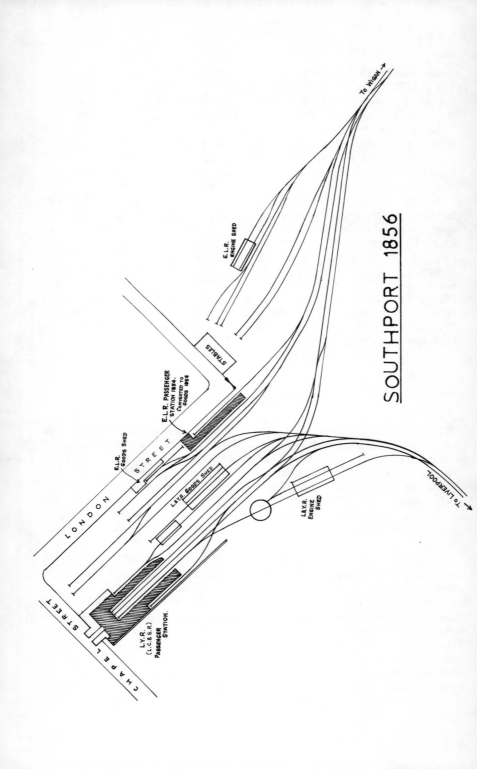

SOUTHPORT 1856

To Wigan

To Liverpool

E.L.R. ENGINE SHED

STABLES

E.L.R. GOODS SHED

E.L.R. PASSENGER STATION 1854. Converted to GOODS 1856

LONDON STREET

L.Y.R. GOODS SHED

L.Y.R. ENGINE SHED

CHAPEL STREET

L.Y.R. (L.C.&S.R.) PASSENGER STATION.

a ledge hewn out of the rock on the north bank, less than ten feet above the river. There was manifestly no room for the railway, and it was decided that the only possible solution was to bore two tunnels, separated by a hollow in the rocks, on the south side of the river. The cost of this work frightened the E.L.R. directors, and it was ordered that the work should not proceed beyond Newchurch station. It was three years before permission was given to go ahead, and a new contract was entered into with Dixon & McKenzie, who quoted a very low figure of £27,845, against Perring's estimate of £47,000. The line was to be single, and included three tunnels, Newchurch No. 1 (162 yards), Newchurch No. 2 (290 yards), and the third a tunnel of 114 yards entering Bacup. Considerable difficulty was experienced with the two Newchurch tunnels, which were through solid rock, but in spite of this the line was completed and opened throughout on 1 October 1852. Bacup station, which was in a somewhat awkward situation owing to the local geography, was at right angles to the line, and approached by a sharp curve immediately beyond the tunnel. The advent of the L.&Y.R. branch from Rochdale in 1881 necessitated some property clearance adjoining the station in order to allow of a similar sharp curve from the opposite direction, and the layout of a small goods yard and engine shed.

For four years the entire branch from Stubbins was operated as a single line, but increasing traffic made it imperative for the line to be doubled. This was carried out in two stages, the first from Stubbins to Rawtenstall being completed by 15 July 1857. Onwards from Rawtenstall there were problems, particularly with the tunnels. The layout of the two Newchurch tunnels precluded any easy way of enlarging them, and so Perring decided to bore a third tunnel through the rock twelve yards to the south. Parliamentary authorisation for the doubling of the Rawtenstall–Bacup section was not obtained until 24 July 1876. Even then, it was two years before any work was done, and 9 March 1881 before it was ready for B.O.T. inspection. As might be expected, it was the new tunnel at Waterfoot which caused all the delay. To get through the spur of the hillside a length of 592 yards was necessary, and as it was all through solid rock, it was by no means easy to bore. Boring and dynamiting went on round the clock for long periods, to the discomfort of the inhabitants of Waterfoot at one end, and Stacksteads at the other. Officially it was to be named Newchurch No. 3, but the workmen had their own name for it—"the thrutch". "Thrutch" is an old and very expressive Lancashire dialect word, which is difficult to explain in standard English; the nearest one can get is possibly "to strive and strain to the limit of one's endurance". This is what the navvies discovered when driving the tunnel, and to them it was always "the thrutch". When the line opened, officialdom, in deference to the local populace and the workforce, adopted the nickname, and the tunnel has been officially Thrutch ever since.

At Bacup, though Hawkshaw had originally planned for a second tunnel alongside the first, Perring found it easier to enlarge the existing bore to take double track, since the ground conditions were much softer than at Waterfoot. The opportunity was taken to rebuild Bacup station at the same time, with some realignment of the trackwork to ease the approach curves. The widened line from Waterfoot to Bacup was eventually opened on 17 March 1881.

From Stubbins the stations on the branch were Ewood Bridge 1¾ miles, Rawtenstall 3½ miles, Cloughfold 4¼ miles, Waterfoot 5¼ miles, Stacksteads 6¼ miles, Bacup 7¾ miles.

CHAPTER 6
Blackburn, Darwen & Bolton Railway

One final addition was made to the E.L.R. system, though it was in the shape of a line owned jointly with the L.&Y.R. This was the former Blackburn, Darwen & Bolton Railway, opened as an independent concern in August 1847, with a five-mile line between Blackburn and Sough, just beyond Darwen, where a temporary terminus was made. Beyond this point the line entered Sough Tunnel (pronounced "suff") which was to become the second longest tunnel on the whole L.&Y.R. system, 2,015 yards. Like Thrutch Tunnel on the Bacup branch, the name Sough was another Lancashire dialect word meaning a drain or sewer, very appropriate again, having regard to the length of the bore, and that several springs and soft layers of clay and sand encountered during its construction made the tunnel very wet in parts. At the southern end a stream had to be diverted by means of a stone trough and a miniature waterfall, into a channel beside the track in the massive cutting, faced with stone, which adjoined the tunnel. At the northern end there was an equally massive cutting. The whole tunnel was on a gradient of 1 in 74 rising towards Bolton, the summit being just beyond the southern entrance, and from here the line descended for 6½ miles into the outskirts of Bolton. Three large viaducts were needed, one of nine 50-foot spans, 120 feet above the Bradshaw Brook (near Entwistle), and two in Bolton itself, where the Rivers Tonge and Croal had to be crossed. The Tonge viaduct, in brick and stone, was nearly half a mile long, and 73 feet above the river. On 4 August 1847 four of the 73 arches collapsed, killing two men. The cause of this was having too few timber centrings for the construction work in hand, and in consequence some of them were moved before the mortar had properly set. The Croal viaduct crossed the small river and the basin of the Manchester, Bolton & Bury Canal, and consisted of six 36-foot stone spans and four 78-foot iron spans on the skew across the basin. Entering Bolton station, the main street (Bradshawgate) was burrowed under, 52 cast iron girders being used to support the roadway. Officially this was classed as a "covered way" 88 yards in length. The line was opened throughout on 12 June 1848.

Sough Tunnel was the scene of a boiler explosion in 1846, while still under construction. The contractor, Evans, was using an old Stockton & Darlington Railway engine, believed to be No. 18 "Shildon", built in 1831, when the boiler exploded just outside the northern entrance of the tunnel. The driver was killed, and the fireman badly burned. Another accident in the tunnel whilst still under construction was caused by the collapse of some wooden staging in one of the vertical shafts from which the work was being carried out; the collapse hurled four navvies to their deaths lower down the shaft. It was found impossible to retrieve their bodies, and the shaft was filled in. The third accident in Sough Tunnel was to contractor's men on 21 December 1880. Work was proceeding to lower the track bed by fifteen inches, in order to give sufficient clearance for Midland Railway trains which were to use the line in the near future. Thirteen men of the day shift were on their way out of the tunnel, having finished work at 6 p.m. when a train from Bolton was heard approaching; the men stepped on to the other track to let it pass, and were immediately mown down by a contractor's locomotive which was bringing some wagons into the tunnel. Two were killed instantly and three were badly injured, one of the three dying later.

North of Blackburn another line, projected by the same company but under a different name, was being organised. Formed by Parliamentary authorisation on 27 July 1846, the Blackburn, Clitheroe & North Western Junction Railway aimed to build a line from Blackburn north-eastwards through Clitheroe and Gisburn to a junction with the North Western Railway (then under construction) at Long Preston. Terence Flanagan was put in charge of the works—as he had been for the Bolton line—and the first sod was cut at Clitheroe by Lord Ribblesdale on 30 December 1846. The original Act proposed a line through Blackburn parallel to the E.L.R., but although this was passed by the Commons, it was vetoed by the Lords, at the instigation of the E.L.R., and the Bill as passed required the Blackburn Railway to pass through the town over E.L.R. metals to Daisyfield Junction at the further end of the tunnel, a distance of ¾ mile, at a toll to be fixed by two arbitrators. Each company was to appoint its own arbitrator, and in the event of a disagreement, a referee would be appointed by the B.O.T. This was very unsatisfactory, and led to much bickering between the parties.

Though on paper the route seemed quite an easy one, this was not borne out in practice. The main problems were posed by the first four miles out of Blackburn. Leaving Daisyfield, first came the Cobwall viaduct, eight stone spans, followed by a massive bridge crossing the main Blackburn–Clitheroe road at a sharp angle, and then a deep cutting and 325-yard tunnel at Wilpshire. Thence forward it was comparatively easy to the valley of the Calder at Whalley, only including a tubular iron bridge of 81 feet span over the same main road at Langho. The Calder valley

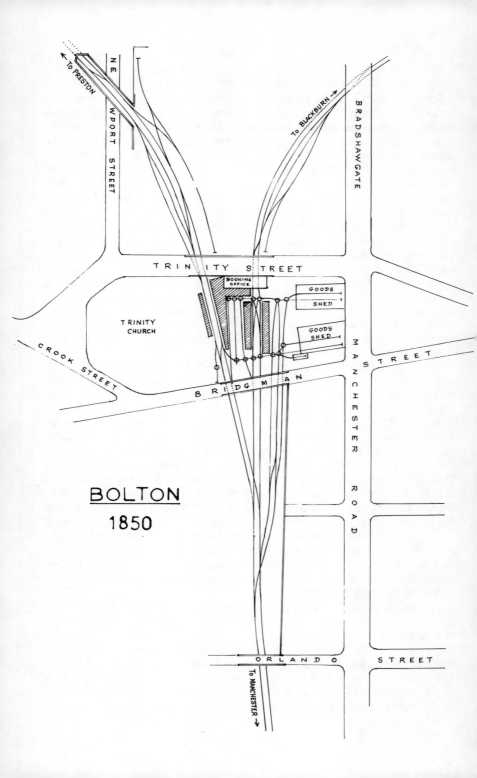

Left: 1848 buildings of Accrington station photographed from the footbridge. The parapets of the viaduct can be seen immediately beyond the platform. Right: 1848 buildings from the rear, just prior to demolition in 1970 (Author)

The Blackburn side of Accrington station about 1910 (Lens of Sutton)

Pleasington station about 1906 (Lens of Sutton)

West Derby station about 1920 (Lens of Sutton)

The original station at Rose Grove, before the 1899 rebuilding

The Aspen Valley timber viaduct, Church, as built in 1848; it was converted to embankment between 1894 and 1925

An early photograph of No. 62, "Memnon".

This early photograph of a Fairbairn 0-4-0 is thought to be E.L.R. No. 24, though it is possibly a Leeds & Manchester Railway engine

An 0-6-0 of the Rossendale class, probably No. 657; domeless boiler, built by Walker in 1853 (F. Moore)

One of the few E.L.R. tank engines. No. 644, "John bull" was built by Walker in 1849 as a tender engine, rebuilt at Bury Works as a side tank in 1864 (F. Moore)

Top: Standard R.&W. Hawthorn 0-4-2 of 1847. Pegasus and Ajax, E.L.R. Nos. 16 & 17, were of this design

Centre: Rossendale class 0-6-0 Agamemnon, No. 656, built by Richard Walker & Bro., 1853; dome on front ring. Below: Charon class 0-6-0 ''Neptune'', No. 687; standard L.&Y.R. 4' 10" goods, built at Miles Platting Works 1866 (F. Moore)

Top: No. 651 "Centaur". Craven class 2-4-0 built at Bury Works 1876 (F. Moore)

Centre: "Pegasus", No. 616. The replacement engine built at Bury Works in 1872 for the original 0-4-2 of 1847 (F. Moore)

Bottom: "Thor", No. 746. Craven class 2-4-0 built at Bury Works in 1876; The last E.L.R. engine in service scrapped 1901 (F. Moore)

The former East Lancashire Railway inspection saloon, built about 1859, and re-numbered 185 in the L.&Y.R. first class list. (Crown Copyright; National Railway Museum)

Colne station as it is today, a single platform with "bus shelter" (Lens of Sutton)

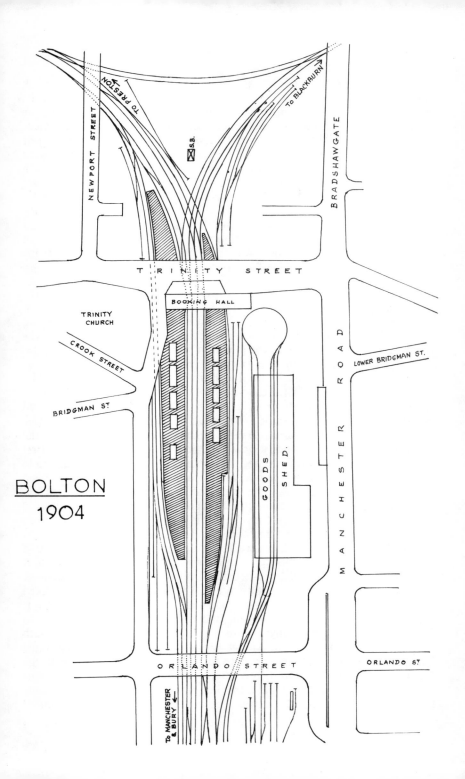

BOLTON
1904

posed another problem, as it was wide and fairly deep, needing a brick viaduct of 48 spans, 70 feet high, and 679 yards in length to get across it. When all but seven of the northern spans had been completed, two of the 41 already built collapsed on 6 October 1849, killing three men. Altogether four million bricks and 436,000 cubic feet of stone had to be used to complete the viaduct. The first 1¾ miles from Daisyfield were continuously uphill, mainly at 1 in 161, but including a short length of 1 in 95 to the summit just beyond Wilpshire, from where there was a continuous fall at 1 in 82 for 4½ miles, including the viaduct, to Whalley. Thence forward, although still generally uphill to the temporary terminus at Chatburn there was one stretch of level track for 1¼ miles, and a final 1 in 120 entering Clitheroe, then continuously at 1 in 178 to Chatburn. Just before entering Clitheroe there was the Primrose viaduct of seven stone arches and one wooden span of 120 feet, which in 1869 was replaced by a further three stone arches.

Money was running short, and bad weather had severely hampered the works, and it was therefore decided to terminate the line at Chatburn for the time being. As it turned out, it was not until the L.&Y.R. obtained an Act in July 1871 permitting them to revive the lapsed powers of the Blackburn Railway but with the junction with the Midland Railway re-sited at Hellifield, that the line was completed.

On 14 June 1850 the line from Blackburn to Chatburn was inspected by Capt. Wynne on behalf of the Board of Trade, and opened for traffic a week later. Then began the trouble. The E.L.R. decided to charge a toll based on six miles for the trains of the B.D.&B.R. passing over the ¾ mile from Bolton Road Junction to Daisyfield Junction. To this extortion the Blackburn company naturally objected, and on the arrival of the first train from Clitheroe on 22 June, they found the junction at Daisyfield blocked, and a force of 200 navvies and a train loaded with stone had been brought up by the E.L.R. The train, after some considerable delay, returned to Clitheroe, and throughout that day only one train was allowed to pass, on payment of the toll. To avoid this impasse, the Blackburn company began turning the passengers off at Daisyfield, out of sight of the E.L.R., and making them walk through the town to Bolton Road station, the train going through empty, without toll. After a few trains had gone through like this, the E.L.R. tumbled to what was happening, and promptly blocked the junction again. The Blackburn company called on Capt. Laws of the L.&Y.R. to intervene, and on 24 June the trains began to run through, but the toll had to be paid, under protest. In addition to this, the company's trains had to pass over the L.&Y.R. south of Bolton to gain access to Manchester, and from Clifton the hated E.L.R. also came into the reckoning again. On 1 April 1850 the Blackburn company entered into an agreement with the L.&Y.R. for certain workings, and possible amalgamation. The amalgamation came to nothing, but the working agreement came into force. Within four or five years, the L.&Y.R. and E.L.R. buried most of their differences and began working in co-operation, albeit a very uneasy one. Amongst the machinations of the two companies, one move proposed by the deputy chairman of the L.&Y.R., William Stuart, was put to running down the Blackburn Railway in order to force amalgamation on it at a very low price. This was accomplished by diverting through traffic from Manchester to Blackburn via Bury and Accrington; and from Wigan to Blackburn via Preston. The Blackburn Railway saw through this piece of skullduggery, and engaged a certain Mr. O'Hagan to survey a route leaving their line by a junction situated between the Tonge and Croal viaducts, and proceeding via Radcliffe, Prestwich and Cheetham Hill into Manchester. A Bill was introduced into Parliament for this independent line on 28 August 1856, and got a favourable hearing on the grounds that it would serve a well-populated area, but the L.&Y.R. successfully opposed the Bill, at a cost of £1000 to themselves. Thereupon the Blackburn Railway sued the L.&Y.R. for £1500 for loss of traffic, and prepared to re-introduce the Bill in the next session of Parliament. The E.L.R. and L.&Y.R. began to get worried over the prospect of an independent line into Manchester, and Stuart offered the Blackburn company half the face value and 4% for the 6% £25 shares of that company, which was rejected out of hand. Thereupon the little company put up a determined fight against its bigger neighbours, by which it earned the plaudits and the respect of not only the railway press, but the Stock Exchange as well. However, it was not to be; though they put up a brave fight, by June 1857 they could fight no longer, and were compelled to agree on 28 November to amalgamation jointly with the L.&Y.R. and E.L.R., which came into effect on 1 January 1858, and was regularised by an L.&Y.R. Act of 12 July of the same year. In 1859—the exact date is not recorded—the B.D.&B.R. station in Bolton Road, Blackburn, was closed, and all trains began using the E.L.R. station.

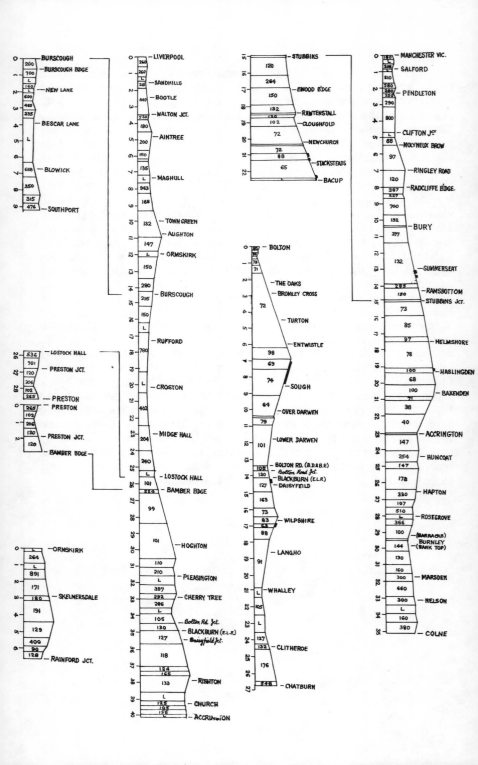

CHAPTER 7
Amalgamation and Later History

The L.N.W.R. line from Salford into Manchester Victoria, over which all L.&Y.R. trains were compelled to pass, had become so congested as to be almost impossible, and in June 1861 the L.&Y.R. obtained Parliamentary permission to construct their own independent line; this was built entirely on viaduct alongside, and to the north of, the L.N.W.R. tracks. It was opened on 1 August 1865, and Salford then became a through station instead of a terminus, though for a hundred years certain East Lancashire Division trains continued to terminate at, or start from, Salford.

Originally Bolton station had been constructed for only one train service, that to Manchester, but by 1850 it was receiving trains from Manchester, Liverpool, Preston and Blackburn, and was hopelessly inadequate. The site was badly restricted, by the bridges of Trinity Street and Bridgman Street, and the retaining walls on either side. The station was enlarged in 1871, but it could only be done by extending the platforms northwards round the curves on to the Preston line on the one hand, and the Blackburn line on the other. This was extremely inconvenient, as it left the junction between the two lines right in the middle of the platforms thus necessitating a good deal of shunting if the junction was not to be permanently blocked. A further Act was obtained on 28 June 1877 to allow the closure of the Bridgman Street bridge and its removal, and widening of Trinity Street and Orlando Street bridges to compensate. The former bridge was dealt with in 1880, and Orlando Street in 1881; these having been completed, Bridgman Street bridge was removed, and both up and down platforms extended 80 yards to the south. Though a great improvement, it was still not entirely satisfactory, as there was a considerable amount of goods traffic passing from the Blackburn line to the Preston line, which could only be done by bringing the trains into the station to reverse. To get rid of this, a curve (known as the Johnson Street Fork) was opened on 26 March 1888, making a triangular junction at the north end, and enabling trains to pass direct from the Blackburn line to the Preston line without entering the station. Finally in 1904 the station was entirely rebuilt, with two island platforms stretching from Trinity Street to Orlando Street, and, by purchase of some old property on the west side, space was made to extend in that direction.

Though the E.L.R. and L.&Y.R. were continually sniping at one another for around ten years, in the middle 1850's they began to see reason, and gradually came to an understanding, culminating finally in amalgamation. The terms of the merger, however, gave the E.L.R. considerable latitude; they still retained their offices and executives at Bury, also the locomotive and carriage works at Bury continued to function. A joint locomotive committee was set up, and under it Sylvester Lees, the E.L.R. locomotive and carriage superintendent, still had a good deal of say. It was agreed that Bury should continue to build passenger engines, whilst goods engines would be supplied by the L.&Y.R. works at Miles Platting. Rather strangely, Bury turned out its first locomotive only after the amalgamation, in 1862; previously the works had only dealt with repairs and rebuilding. From then until the works were closed down in 1886, 16 locomotives were built, all 2-4-0's, and all except four to the same design which Lees developed from the original Sharp pattern of 1848–1850. These will be dealt with more fully in the chapter on rolling stock. When J.A.F. Aspinall became Chief Mechanical Engineer of the L.&Y.R. in 1885, and the new Horwich locomotive works were planned, both Bury and Miles Platting works were singled out for closure, which took place when Horwich opened in 1887. Bury became a store until 1916, when it became a repair shop for the Manchester District electric stock.

Under the L.&Y.R., the East Lancashire lines became known as the East Lancashire Division, with which was incorporated the former L.&Y.R. Burnley–Todmorden branch. In 1860 the rather astonishing decision was made to transfer the headquarters of the Division from Bury to Accrington. How they managed to fit the offices into the very restricted accommodation at Accrington, after the spaciousness of Bury, is a complete mystery, since no additional building was available, or even contemplated. However, Accrington remained the Divisional headquarters until well after the new station was built there in 1882. James Smithells, who was passenger superintendent for the E.L. Division, was an extremely popular figure in Accrington. He did much for the people and businessmen of the town, and it was with universal regret that he left to become general manager of the L.&Y.R. in 1864. In 1913 it was decided to set up a centralised control at Manchester Victoria, and all the divisional offices were abolished.

The E.L. Division was a fairly prosperous one, and carried some intensive traffic, both passenger and goods, with the latter slightly predominating. It used to be said that the signal arms on Baxenden bank were in a state of perpetual motion, so great was the traffic up and down it. A good deal of traffic was routed from Yorkshire via Todmorden and Accrington to Manchester or Liverpool, to ease the congestion on the main line via Summit Tunnel and Rochdale. The E.L.R. lines were difficult to work, owing to the steep gradients, and banking engines were constantly in use from Accrington or Ramsbottom to Baxenden summit, and from Bolton or Blackburn to Entwistle, likewise from Todmorden or Rosegrove to Copy Pit. By agreement with the Midland Railway, in 1885 that company's through expresses from Liverpool or Manchester to Glasgow began to work over the E.L. Division via Blackburn to Hellifield. In return, the L.&Y.R. was granted certain running powers over Midland lines, notably from Colne to Skipton and Bradford, via Ilkley; also from Hellifield to Ingleton and Wennington for excursions. The greatest traffic over the Division was during the summer months, with numerous special excursion trains from Yorkshire to Blackpool and Southport, culminating in the "Wakes Weeks" (July and most of August), when the entire towns of East Lancashire used to close down in turn for a week's holiday, and thousands of passengers besieged the local stations. Not only Blackpool and Southport were catered for; special trains were put on (mainly on Friday nights) to such faraway places as Torquay, Bournemouth, Folkestone, Yarmouth, Scarborough, Edinburgh, Glasgow, and a dozen or more Welsh resorts. The author can remember Accrington station crammed with passengers on all platforms, and the crowd spilling over from the booking hall right down the station approach on these occasions. Those days, unhappily, have gone and will never return.

After the Second World War, traffic never recovered to its former level, and eventually Dr. Beeching was brought in to rationalise the railways. Under his general recommendations, the E.L.R. main line from Clifton Junction to Accrington was closed completely on 5 December 1966, after operating a shuttle service between Accrington and Bury only for two years. About the same time the Midland line from Colne to Skipton also closed completely, severing a valuable link between Lancashire towns and Leeds, and with the Rosegrove—Todmordon branch retained for goods only, there remained but the Manchester—Rochdale—Todmorden line as a link between the two counties. The Blackburn—Hellifield line closed to passenger service on 10 September 1962, but still remains in use for goods service, reduced to single line, and at a reduced speed owing to trouble with Whalley viaduct. On odd occasions it has been used as a relief through route when work has had to be done on the West Coast main line. From Stubbins to Accrington and Rawtenstall to Bacup were dismantled in 1970/71, but the section between Bury and Rawtenstall was singled and retained for the weekly coal train which supplied the East Lancashire coal depot at Rawtenstall. This also has now gone, and the line lies derelict, but with the hope that some arrangement can be made between British Rail and the East Lancashire Preservation Society for its purchase and eventual re-opening. Parts of the Accrington—Stubbins trackbed have been incorporated into a new road, as has also the section between Rawtenstall and Cloughfold.

Most of the stations on the former E.L.R. lines have been dismantled and converted to unmanned halts, with the exception of Bury, Blackburn, Burnley Central and Nelson. Blackburn has had its inner platforms cut back to half their length, and the Skelmersdale branch has been completely dismantled down to Rainford and St. Helens. The Southport branch remains in use, with its stations reduced to halts, and the junctions at Burscough taken out. Another casualty of the Beeching Report was the direct line from Bamber Bridge to Preston, which was closed in 1970. From this time onwards, trains from Blackburn to Preston reverted to the old route via Lostock Hall and Farington Curve, slightly over two miles longer. This closure cleared the way for the complete dismantling of the

E.L.R. side of Preston station and the Butler Street goods yard. The parts of the old E.L.R. which still remain—Preston to Colne, Bolton to Hellifield, and Ormskirk to Preston, were divested of all signal boxes, and are now operated electronically from the vast new signal box at Preston. The E.L.R. has taken a beating, but it is not yet completely dead, though there is not much hope for its survival in the years to come.

CHAPTER 8
Locomotives

The locomotive history of the E.L.R. was complicated and controversial. In spite of diligent research by several eminent historians there are some points which are still not definitely settled. Amongst these must be included the locomotive boiler details, of which there appear to be at least three versions, and which is correct is anybody's guess. One version is given in the table, but it is emphasised that it should be taken with reserve.

On the formation of the E.L.R. in 1846 an order was given to Richard Walker & Brother, of Bury, for forty locomotives of two basic types, 2-2-2 and 2-4-0, to be delivered as and when required over a period of five years. This order was later revised, at Walker's request, to twenty. Why this order was given in the first place is a mystery, for Walker's had never previously built a locomotive, and after the completion of the contract never built another. The works was certainly incapable of constructing boilers and dealing with heavy castings, being a small general engineering plant, and although diligent enquiries have been carried through, there appears to be no definite data as to how the locomotive building was carried out. Richard Walker was a director of the E.L.R., so no doubt there was a connection here somewhere, with the placing of the order. All engines built by Walker were basically to Sharp Bros. design, no doubt the working drawings supplied by Sharp's to the E.L.R. were either copied for, or the originals passed on to, Walker's. As delivered, Walker's locomotives were distinguishable from Sharp's only by their somewhat crude finish. Where the boilers, cylinders and other heavy parts originated is a mystery; they could possibly have been supplied by Sharp's, or the other Manchester firm of locomotive engineers, Fairbairns, but there is no confirmation.

Sylvester Lees took charge of the locomotive department in 1848, and proved a capable engineer, holding the post until his death on 22 March 1865. He was succeeded by John Jacques, who was appointed Outdoor Superintendent, with Henry Critchley as Indoor Superintendent (on the L.&Y.R. system of divided responsibility for locomotives). Critchley died in September 1867, and his place was taken by George Roberts. The E.L.R. established a small works alongside the line and adjoining the engine shed, about ¼ mile south of Bury station, in the district of the town known as Buckley Wells. Here the repair and rebuilding of locomotives took place, also carriages and wagons were produced. Building *new* locomotives did not commence at Bury until 1862, after the amalgamation with the L.&Y.R., though some of the rebuilds turned out prior to this were virtually new engines. Lees adhered to the basics of Sharp's designs, outside sandwich frames, curved above the driving axles, domes on the front ring of the boiler, and raised fireboxes. Salter safety valves, mounted one pair on the dome and one pair on the firebox, were the rule, though in the late 1850's the dome-mounted valves were eliminated. Certain locomotives also came out from time to time with the dome on the middle ring of the boiler. After the amalgamation, details changed; flush fireboxes with Naylor safety valves and closed domes became the rule. A joint locomotive committee was set up, and it was agreed that Bury should build passenger engines, whilst goods engines should be supplied by the Miles Platting works of the L.&Y.R. Until 1875 no number plates were fitted to either L.&Y.R. or E.L.R. locomotives, but in that year, with the arrival of Barton Wright to take charge of the L.&Y.R. locomotive department, the standard oval number plate was designed. From 1875, 600 was added to the E.L.R. numbers, to integrate the stock into one list. By this time the highest E.L.R. number was 146, though at least half the numbers were taken by Miles Platting-built goods engines of two or three different classes. E.L.R. name plates were fixed to the centre of the boiler on each side, and had raised brass letters and edges. Numbers were probably allotted as the engines were delivered; there seems to have been little attempt to group numbers into classes.

Medusa class

Four engines by Richard Walker, Bury, 1846. These were the first engines ordered against the contract with Walker. They were of Sharp's earlier standard design, in which the upper edge of the outside sandwich frames had a sharp curve over the driving axle, in contrast to later examples which had a curved edge of considerably greater radius. The boiler was in three rings, with dome on the middle ring, and Salter safety valves on top. A second lock-up valve was fitted on the firebox, and the dome had a square base. At least one of the class, *MEDUSA*, was rebuilt prior to 1853 as a 2-4-0 side tank with 5'0" coupled wheels, and later Walker's were asked to rebuild the other three similarly, but there is great doubt as to whether this was actually carried out. The driving wheels were 5'6", carrying wheels 3'6", inside cylinders 13" × 18". The internal boiler dimensions probably varied with each engine.

No.	Name	Built	Rebuilt	Withdrawn
1	MEDUSA	1846	1852(?) 2-4-OT	1/1867
3	HECATE	"	?	1/1867
10	DIOMED	"	?	4/1869
18	LYNX	1847	?	9/1867

No. 10 was exchanged in 1862 for a L.Y.R. outside-cylindered Hawkshaw single (L.&Y. 90) which took the same name and number.

Roach class

Four engines by Fenton & Craven, Leeds 1846. A very unsatisfactory class. Six were ordered in March 1845, and a further six in March 1846, but in the event the E.L.R. took delivery of only four. How they got out of taking the other eight is not known, but they were certainly glad they had got only four. These engines were built as outside-cylindered 2-2-2's of Stephenson long-boiler type (i.e., all wheels in front of the firebox). They had inside frames, wheels 3'6" and 5'6", cylinders 15" × 20". The boilers were 13'0" long, domeless, and in four rings; fireboxes of the "haystack" pattern with safety valves on top. In service they were very unsatisfactory, having a motion which was described as "diabolical", pitching and swaying to an alarming degree. In 1848 they were sent to Hawthorn's for rebuilding as 2-4-0's, in which process the wheelbase was lengthened, and the boilers shortened to 10'0", at a cost of £500 each. Some ten years later they were again rebuilt as inside-cylindered 0-6-0's with 4'9" wheels. In this form they were much better, and lasted until the 1870's.

No.	Name	Built	2-4-0	Rebuilt 0-6-0	Withdrawn
2	ROACH	1846	1848	1858	3/1875
4	SPITFIRE	"	"	1852	6/1878
5	CYCLOPS	"	"	1859	3/1876
6	SALAMANDER	"	"	1858	3/1875

Bacchus class

Four engines by Sharp Bros., Manchester, 1846. These were ordered by the Blackburn & Preston Railway. They were similar to the Medusa class, but had the larger radius curve of the frames above the driving axle, and were larger, with a longer wheelbase, 5'0" driving wheels, and 15" × 20" cylinders.

No.	Name	Built	Works No.	Rebuilt 2-4-0	Withdrawn
7	BACCHUS	1846	337	1866	11/1873
8	JUPITER	"	350	1869	5/1876
9	VESTA	"	353	1865	11/1873
11	MERCURY	"	354	1869	9/1877

Samson class

Five engines by Haigh Foundry, Wigan 1847. 0-6-0 goods engines of a more-or-less standard Haigh Foundry design, with 4'9" wheels, 15" × 24" cylinders, and long boilers, though they looked less ungainly than the Roach class. The boilers had four rings, with dome on the second; the dome had a square base, and Salter safety valves on top. An ornamental cover on the firebox carried another spring balance valve. Frames and cylinders were inside. A sixth Haigh Foundry engine was No. 23, *Elk*; also built in 1847. Nothing is known about this engine, but it is believed to have been a 2-2-2. It was rebuilt in 1859, and put up for sale as "worn out" in 1867.

No.	Name	Built	Rebuilt	Withdrawn
12	SAMSON	1847	1857	12/1870
13	ZAMIEL	"	1855	6/1878
19	HERCULES	"	?	3/1875
20	VULCAN	"	?	4/1875
22	ATLAS	"	1856	4/1875

Aurora class

Five engines by Sharp Bros., Manchester, 1847−1849. Very similar to the earlier Bacchus class, having boilers of the same dimensions, but varied in having a shorter wheelbase and 5′6″ wheels. *Aeolus* and *Prometheus* were rebuilt as 2-4-0's, but *Sunbeam* always remained a 2-2-2. *Phantom* may have been rebuilt as a 2-4-0 at an earlier date, but in April 1876 it was completely renewed at Bury as a 2-4-0 of the Craven class. *Aurora* became a 2-2-2 side tank in June 1854.

No.	Name	Built	Works No.	Rebuilt		Withdrawn
14	AURORA	1847	396	1854	2-2-2T	11/1873
15	AEOLUS	"	398	1868	2-4-0	2/1880
21	PROMETHEUS	"	439	1870	2-4-0	4/1880
37	SUNBEAM	1849	578	1865	2-2-2	12/1873
38	PHANTOM	"	579			3/1876

Pegasus class

Two engines by R.&W. Hawthorn, Newcastle. Two 0-4-2 goods engines purchased in 1847. These had 5′0″ coupled wheels and outside frames, which had the hornplates made separately and bolted on outside. Inside cylinders had Hawthorn's standard 21″ stroke, with 15″ diameter. The boiler was in three rings, with dome in the centre, this dome being of a pattern peculiar to the makers, resembling an overgrown stew pot, complete with lid, and even a knob on top. Safety valves were on the raised firebox. In 1863 both engines were (nominally) rebuilt, becoming 2-4-0's. It is very likely that there was little, if anything, of the original engines in the "rebuilds", for they had the standard E.L.R. frames, Craven class boilers, 5′6″ coupled wheels, and 15″ × 20″ inside cylinders. In their rebuilt form, they were indistinguishable from the Craven class.

No.	Name	Built	Works No.	Rebuilt	Withdrawn
16	PEGASUS	1847	606	1863 2-4-0	2/1885
17	AJAX	"	607	1863 2-4-0	6/1870

Goliath class

Five engines by Fairbairn & Co., Manchester 1848/9. In May 1848 an enquiry was put out by the E.L.R. board for a locomotive suitable for banking duties on Baxenden bank. Almost at once Fairbairn's sent an engine for trial, and after testing it out thoroughly, Sylvester Lees pronounced it satisfactory for the purpose, and it was taken into stock.

Four more of the same design were ordered, and were delivered in 1849. These five engines have been the subject of much controversy, but it seems almost certain, in the light of Mr. E. Craven's researches, that they were 0-4-0 tender engines of Edward Bury's pattern, of which at that time Fairbairn's were building a number for the L.&Y.R. They had all the usual Bury features, bar frames, domeless boilers, and "haystack" fireboxes which had a pair of spring balance safety valves mounted on top in a fore-and-aft position. The coupling rods were of circular section, and, unlike the prototype Bury engines, a running plate and small splashers were fitted. Apart from *Hurricane*, which was withdrawn in 1869, they lasted until the middle 1870's, mainly on banking duties from Accrington and Ramsbottom.

No.	Name	Built	Withdrawn
24	GOLIATH	1848	4/1875
32	ACHILLES	1849	5/1876
35	HECTOR	"	5/1876
39	HURRICANE	"	5/1869
41	THUNDERER	"	5/1876

Venus class.
Ten engines by Walker's, Bury, 1848–1850. The standard passenger engines of the E.L.R. at the earlier period, and virtually the Aurora class with a lengthened wheelbase. All were built out of Walker's contract, and it seems likely that some of the larger components were provided by Sharp's. They were good engines, but were spoilt by being poorly finished. Three of the class remained as singles throughout their life, but the others were rebuilt to 2-4-0's, being then identical with the Phaeton class, except for a wheelbase one foot shorter. They had 5'6" driving wheels, 3'9" carrying wheels, and 15" × 20" cylinders.

No.	Name	Built	Rebuilt	Withdrawn
25	VENUS	1848	1864 2-2-2	9/1873
26	LIGHTNING	"	1865 2-4-0	4/1882
27	CAMILLA	"	1870 2-4-0	2/1881
28	LUCIFER	"	1868 2-4-0	6/1878
29	ARIEL	"	1868 2-4-0	8/1880
31	ORION	"	1864	9/1882
49	GAZELLE	1850	1868 2-4-0	9/1880
50	BANSHEE	"	1868	10/1873
53	VIVID	"	1870 2-4-0	6/1880
54	REINDEER	"	1873 2-4-0	10/1880

Phaeton class
Four engines by Walker's, Bury, 1848/9 and two engines by Sharp's, Manchester, 1849. These were the basis of the standard E.L.R. passenger engines. They were built as 2-4-0's, with a wheelbase one foot longer than the Venus class, and a larger boiler which became the standard for all future 2-4-0's. At rebuilding, most of the 2-2-2's were fitted with the same

boiler, and apart from differences in wheelbase, were assimilated into the Phaeton class. The engines had the curved outside framing typical of Sharp's design, 5'6" coupled wheels, 3'9" leading wheels, and inside cylinders 16" × 20". Though all the boilers had the same dimensions, tubes, and heating surfaces, the position of the dome varied, mostly on the front ring, but some in the middle. Slightly raised fireboxes were fitted, with spring balance safety valves on top. As reboilered, all had flush fireboxes with Naylor safety valves, and once again there was variation in the position of the dome. Latterly these 2-4-0's were the mainstay of the E.L.R. services, and after the amalgamation some of them migrated across the border into Yorkshire, where they did good work around Bradford, Leeds, and Goole.

No.	Name	Maker	Works No.	Built	Rebuilt	Withdrawn
30	PHAETON	Walker		1848	11/1864	9/1880
33	MAZEPPA	"		1849	2/1870	6/1878
34	TAMERLANE	Sharp	574	"	3/1867	3/1878
36	MILO	"	575	"	3/1863	6/1878
40	FIRE KING	Walker		"	12/1870	9/1882
42	VAMPIRE	"		"	7/1867	7/1878

John Bull class

Two engines by Walker's, Bury 1849/50; and two by Sharp's, Manchester, 1850; ordered for goods traffic, having 5'0" coupled wheels, but otherwise identical with the Phaeton class. In 1864 and 1865, the two Walker engines were rebuilt to 2-4-0 side tanks, for which the coupled axle springs were removed from above the running plate and underhung. A bunker holding 2 tons of coal was fitted behind the footplate, the main frames having extension pieces bolted on to support it. A small open-backed cab was fitted, these probably being the first engines to have cabs. The side tanks held 920 gallons of water. Neither of the Sharp engines was rebuilt.

No.	Name	Maker	Works No.	Built	Rebuilt	Withdrawn
44	JOHN BULL	Walker		1849	12/1864	9/1880
45	CALIBAN	"		"	1/1865	9/1880
51	CENTAUR	Sharp	651	1850		6/1876
52	GORGON	"	657	"		5/1876

Iron Duke class

One engine by Sharp Bros., Manchester, 1850 and one by Fawcett, Preston & Co., Liverpool 1847. These two engines are classed together, since they were basically the same, varying only in details. The design was Sharp's, and was almost identical with several engines supplied to the Manchester, Sheffield & Lincolnshire Railway at the same period. Fawcett, Preston's engine was built in an attempt to break into the loco-motive market, and is thought to have actually been built in 1847, but no purchaser could be found, and the firm were glad to sell it off at a reduced price in 1850 to the E.L.R. Its name, *Phoenix*, was the company's trade mark. Both engines were long-boiler 0-6-0's, with inside frames, 4'9" wheels, and inside cylinders 18" × 24", making them much more powerful than any other E.L.R. locomotive. The boilers were in four rings with dome on the second ring, and a pair of Salter safety valves over the firebox in a casing similar to Midland Railway practice. The main frames were slotted out in Sharp's engine, but *Phoenix* had tie bars between the hornplates. Both were rebuilt with cylinders lined up to 16" diameter at about the same time, and were withdrawn together in 1880.

No.	Name	Makers	Works No.	Built	Rebuilt	Withdrawn
43	PHOENIX	Fawcett, Preston		1847	12/1869	9/1880
46	IRON DUKE	Sharp	639	1850	1/1870	9/1880

Pluto class
Two engines by Sharp Bros., Manchester 1850. At the same time that *Iron Duke* was purchased, two smaller goods engines of the 0-4-2 arrangement were obtained from Sharp's, of the makers' standard design. Rather unusually for this wheel arrangement, the wheelbase was equally divided. They were simple locomotives, with inside frames and cylinders, three-ring boiler with dome in the centre, and raised firebox. Coupled wheels were 4'9" and trailing wheels 3'6"; cylinders 15" × 22". *Pluto* was fitted with a new firebox in 1857, but was not otherwise rebuilt.

No.	Name	Maker	Works No.	Built	Withdrawn
47	PLUTO	Sharp	642	1850	5/1876
48	CERBERUS	"	643	"	12/1870

Rossendale class
Four engines by Walker's, Bury, 1852/3; the last engines built by Walker, and ordered additional to, but not part of, the original contract. They were unlike any of the previous Walker engines, being long-boiler 0-6-0's, based on the Iron Duke design, and were the most unprepossessing machines the firm had built, which was saying something. Whether the four boilers were obtained from the same source or not is doubtful, for no two of them seemed to be alike. *Rossendale* had a domeless boiler, the dome being placed on the firebox; *Agamemnon* had a dome on the front ring, while *Dugdale* had the dome on the second ring. The type of boiler on *Hannibal* has not been established. In all cases the dome carried a pair of Salter safety valves. Wheels were 4'9" diameter and inside cylinders 15" × 24", with inside frames. All were rebuilt with 16" × 24" cylinders, but retained their original boilers.

No.	Name	Makers	Built	Rebuilt	Withdrawn
55	ROSSENDALE	Walker	12/1852	3/1873	9/1882
56	AGAMEMNON	"	1/1853	1/1868	7/1881
57	HANNIBAL	"	7/1853	10/1874	9/1882
58	DUGDALE	"	2/1854	2/1870	7/1881

Ulysses class

Five engines by Stothert & Slaughter, Bristol. 1856; with their "haystack" fireboxes, which must have been the last of their type built, these 0-6-0's appeared rather archaic, even for 1856. They had inside frames, wheels 4′9″ diameter, and inside cylinders 16″ × 24″. The boilers were domeless, and the safety valves were perched on top of the firebox. Only two were rebuilt. One source states that *Sphinx* was fitted with 4′0″ diameter wheels at some later time, but this is not borne out by L.&Y.R. records.

No.	Name	Maker	Works No.	Built	Rebuilt	Withdrawn
59	ULYSSES	Slaughter	330	7/1856	6/1868	6/1876
60	SPHINX	"	329	"	10/1874	9/1882
61	NESTOR	"	331	8/1856		8/1881
62	MEMNON	"	332	"		5/1877
63	SESTOSTRIS	"	333	"		2/1880

Giraffe class

Two engines by Beyer, Peacock & Co., Manchester, 1857; 2-4-0's substantially of London & South Western Railway design, and embodying Joseph Beattie's patent firebox and combustion chamber. Just why the E.L.R. purchased them is not clear, for they were not cheap, they cost £5100 each. They could have been part of a cancelled order for the L.&S.W.R., since five of them were in the same batch, two going to the Egyptian State Railways, and the fifth to the Glasgow & South Western Railway. They were somewhat ungainly machines, this perhaps being emphasised by their length, and the fact that at 5′10″ they had the lowest pitched boilers of any E.L.R. locomotives. The coupled wheels were 6′0″ diameter, and the cylinders were outside, placed in front of the leading axle. The boiler was 10′4″ long and contained a combustion chamber 4′9″ long at the firebox end, giving a tube length of only 5′4″, while the firebox contained a midfeather, giving the effect of having two fireboxes —indeed, they were fitted with two firedoors. Another unusual feature was that the connecting rods were fitted inside the coupling rods. In 1866 they were exchanged with the L.&Y.R. for two Hawkshaw 2-4-0's (Nos. 85 and 86) and in 1869 were rebuilt at Miles Platting with domeless boilers of Yates' design.

No.	Name	Maker	Works No.	Built	Rebuilt	Withdrawn
65	GIRAFFE	B. Peacock	70	1857	1869	11/1878
66	ANTELOPE	"	71	"	"	8/1879

Charon class

Two engines built by L.&Y.R. (Miles Platting) 1857–1859. Before the amalgamation, the L.&Y.R. transferred two of Jenkins' standard 4′10″ 0-6-0's to the E.L.R. Subsequently 28 further engines of the class were built at Miles Platting expressly for the East Lancashire Division, and further purely L.&Y.R. locomotives of three different classes were also built for the Division. As these were never purely E.L.R. stock, it is not proposed to deal with them in detail.

The Charon class were inside framed engines, with 4' 10" wheels and 15" × 24" inside cylinders. The boilers had domes on the middle ring, these being of Jenkins' peculiar "cottage loaf" design, and the spring balance safety valves were in a tall casing on the firebox. No. 64, *Charon*, was built in July 1857, rebuilt in July 1871, and withdrawn in July 1881; No. 67, *Macedon* was built in May 1859, rebuilt in December 1874, and also withdrawn in July 1881. The other 28, and the subsequent engines of other classes, were given E.L.R. list numbers and names.

Craven class

Twelve engines built by E.L.R. at Bury, 1862–1877. Developed from the Phaeton class, with a longer wheelbase and the flush firebox boiler of the John Bull rebuilds, these were the best engines the company had. Though the earlier ones were built with weather-boards only, all of them (including the earlier classes) were fitted with small cabs of the L.N.W.R. type in the seventies. Outside frames, curved over the coupled axles, were used, with 5' 6" wheels and inside cylinders 16" × 20", though some had 22" or 24" stroke. The position of the domes varied, some being on the front ring of the boiler, and some on the centre ring, but owing to boiler changes, it is not possible to sort out which engines had each type. The last engine built, No. 662, came out without a name, and its L.&Y.R. number; probably the previous two engines also received L.&Y.R. numbers when built. Three engines (the Clio sub-class) were built as 2-4-0 side tanks, almost identical with the John Bull rebuilds, but were converted to tender engines within two years. The E.L.R. apparently had not much use for tank engines. An odd engine, No. 113 *Juno*, was built in 1871 from spare parts and a reconditioned boiler; it was considerably smaller than the rest. *Thor*, No. 746, had the distinction of being the very last E.L.R. engine in service; it was not withdrawn until 1901. Only four of the twelve were actually additions to capital stock, the others were replacements of older engines scrapped.

No.	Name	Maker	Built	Rebuilt	Withdrawn
73	BLACKLOCK	E.L.R.	3/1862	3/1871	11/1882
80	CRAVEN	"	9/1863	2/1877	11/1892
1	ODIN	"	1/1867	1869*	8/1882
3	CLIO	"	1/1867	1869*	8/1882
18	TITAN	"	9/1867	1869*	11/1882
113	JUNO	"	10/1871		2/1886
16	PEGASUS	"	1/1872		2/1886
146	THOR	"	1/1876		2/1901
38	PHANTOM	"	4/1876		10/1892
608	JUPITER	"	5/1876		5/1893
651	CENTAUR	"	6/1876		8/1892
662	—	"	5/1877		2/1898

*Built as tank engines; rebuilt to tender engines at this date.

The E.L.R. locomotive livery was dark green, lined in black and white, with red-brown outside frames, polished brass domes and safety valve covers.

CHAPTER 9
Passenger Rolling Stock

Not a great deal is known. It is stated in sources that early railway carriages were modelled on those of the Manchester & Leeds Railway, first class coaches being painted dark blue, and second and third classes "in lighter shades"—whatever that may mean. From a stock return issued in January 1850, the rolling stock at the close of 1849 comprised 21 first class, 42 second class, 61 third class, and 7 composites, plus 6 "coupe carriages" (? saloons), and 14 parcel & luggage vans. With three carriage trucks and five horse boxes, this gave a total of 159 vehicles in passenger stock. Goods vehicles at the same time totalled 692, all open. When the joint locomotive committee was formed in 1857, the E.L.R. reported that it had 50 first class, 70 second class, 77 third class, and 20 composite carriages; 2 carriage trucks, 12 horse boxes, 21 parcels and luggage vans, total 252. The goods vehicles comprised 1743 open wagons, 26 goods vans, and 24 brake vans.

James Newall was appointed Carriage & Wagon Superintendent in 1848, and it was not long before he was designing his own coaches, of which a number were built in the E.L.R. works at Bury, and others obtained from outside contractors. Newall's coaches were mainly four-wheeled, though he had produced a few six-wheeled coaches by the time of the amalgamation in 1859. Carriages were built at Bury till 1876, after which all carriage and wagon work was transferred to the newly-opened Newton Heath works of the L.&Y.R. The coaches produced by Newall varied from 18 feet to 26 feet in length for four-wheelers, and 30 to 32 feet for six-wheelers. They had low arc roofs, square-cornered side mouldings, and curved tops to windows and vertical panels. With these features they were difficult to distinguish at first sight from Charles Fay's coaches for the L.&Y.R. The main distinguishing feature between the two companies was in the brake vans; Newall preferred the guard's lookout duckets and roof "birdcage" in the centre, while Fay preferred them at one end. A few samples of Newall's coaches are illustrated in the line drawings. Nothing has come to light concerning numbering of passenger stock.

One peculiar vehicle, running on four wheels, was built in either 1858 or 1859, this being a carriage for official purposes, and generally referred to as the "Inspection Saloon". It was 21 feet long over headstocks and 8 feet wide. At each end was a short verandah with seats against the end bulkheads and an iron railing across the ends. The central portion consisted of a saloon with a single door in the centre of each side, and seats for eight persons arranged round two small tables. In the end bulkheads, a door led onto the open verandah. There were two large windows in each side, with straight tops, but rounded corners. The most unusual feature was the solebars, which were curved downwards in a semicircle in the centre, allowing a dropped floor in the doorways. In addition there was a full-length footboard on each side with an extra step below the door, to provide easy access from rail level. A vertical brake shaft, operated by a handwheel, was fitted on each verandah, and at one end only a roof seat was fitted, rather an anachronism for that period. This remarkable vehicle was later fitted with vacuum brakes, and numbered 185 in the L.&Y.R. first class list; it was in regular use until 1922, when it was withdrawn. It was the only E.L.R. vehicle to be accorded a place in the L.&Y.R. Diagram Book (Diagram 23). One or two other E.L.R. vehicles survived until shortly after the 1923 Grouping, in departmental stock, and one six-wheeled brake van (numbered 166 in the L.&Y.R. van list) ran until the mid 1920's as a mail van between Preston and Burnley.

James Newall is perhaps best known for his mechanical brake gear, patented in 1852, and which he fitted to about half the E.L.R. passenger stock. A two-inch diameter shaft ran along the coach roof, connected between coaches by square shafts working inside a square tube. A wheel in the guard's van was arranged to rotate the shafts by suitable gearing, and a rack and pinion working against a spring applied the brakes on each coach. The brake was officially tested on Baxenden bank on 22 October 1853. A train of seven coaches was brought to rest from 35 m.p.h. on the 1 in 40 gradient in 228 yards. Further tests were carried out on 9 November, several eminent engineers being present: Francis Trevithick and Samuel Worthington of the L.N.W.R., Hurst of the L.&Y.R., and some of the directorate of the E.L.R. This time the test train had ten coaches, and was brought to rest from 40 m.p.h. by the efforts of one man, in 138 yards. A similar train fitted with ordinary hand brakes needs 800 yards to stop, using two men. Charles Fay conceived a similar brake on the L.&Y.R., with a shaft running under the coach floor, and working the brakes through a worm wheel and quadrant. After the amalgamation, Fay and Newall worked together to perfect this brake gear, which eventually showed up well in the Newark brake trials of 1873. The train which crashed near Helmshore in 1860 was, unfortunately, not fitted with Newall's brake.

LOCOMOTIVE LIST.

Name	Type	Wheels	Cyls.	Makers	Works No	Built	Rebuilt	W'drawn	Class	
Medusa	2-2-2	5'0"	13x18	W		9/1846	1853 2-4-0T	1/67	Medusa	
Roach	"	5'6" 0	15x20	FC		10/"	1848 2-4-0 1858 0-6-0 4'9"	3/75	Roach	
Hecate	"	5'0"	13x18	W		5/"	1854 2-4-0T (?)	1/67	Medusa	
Spitfire	"	5'6" 0	15x20	FC		9/"	1848 2-4-0 1852 0-6-0 4'9"	6/78	Roach	
Cyclops	"	"	"	"		"	" 1858 "	3/76	"	
Salamander	"	"	"	"		"	" 1859 "	3/75	"	
Bacchus	"	"	15x20	S	337	5/"	1866 2-4-0	6/72	Bacchus	
Jupiter	"	"	"	"	350	6/"	1869 2-4-0	5/76	"	
Vesta	"	"	"	"	353	"	1865 2-4-0	6/72	"	
Diomed	"	5'0"	13x18	W		12/"	1854 2-4-0T(?)	4/69	Medusa	To LYR 90/42
Mercury	"	5'6"	15x20	S	354	8/"	1869 2-4-0	4/77	Bacchus	
Samson	0-6-0	4'9"	15x24	HF		3/1847	1857	12/70	Samson	
Zamiel	"	"	"	"		12/"	3/1855	6/78	"	
Aurora	2-2-2	5'0"	15x20	S	396	3/"	1854 2-2-2T	11/73	Aurora	
Aeolus	"	"	"	"	398	3/"	3/1868 2-4-0	2/80	"	
Pegasus	0-4-2	5'0"	15x21	H	606	4/"	1863 2-4-0	12/71	Pegasus	
Ajax	"	"	"	"	607	"	1863 2-4-0	6/70	"	
Lynx	2-2-2	5'0"	13x18	W		5/"	1854 2-4-0T(?)	9/67	Medusa	
Hercules	0-6-0	4'9"	15x24	HF		"		3/75	Samson	
Vulcan	"	"	"	"		7/"		4/75	"	
Prometheus	2-2-2	5'6"	15x20	S	439	9/"	1862 2-4-0 9/1870	4/80	Aurora	
Atlas	0-6-0	4'9"	15x24	HF		11/"	1856	4/75	Samson	
Elk	2-2-2(?)			"		7/1848	5/1859	11/67	Elk	
Goliath	0-4-0	4'9"	15x24	F		5/"		4/75	Goliath	
Venus	2-2-2	5'6"	15x20	W		6/"	1864	9/73	Venus	
Lightning	"	"	"	"		"	6/1865 2-4-0	9/82	"	
Camilla	"	"	"	"		"	12/1870 2-4-0	7/81	"	
Lucifer	"	"	"	"		9/"	9/1868 2-4-0	6/78	"	
Ariel	"	"	"	"		10/"	10/1868 2-4-0	8/80	"	
Phaeton	2-4-0	"	"	"		11/"	11/1864	9/80	Phaeton	
Orion	"	"	"	"		12/"	12/1864	9/82	"	
Achilles	0-4-0	4'9"	15x24	F		3/1849		5/76	Goliath	
Mazeppa	2-2-2	5'6"	15x20	W		"	7/1870 2-4-0	4/78	Venus	
Tamerlane	2-4-0	"	"	S	574	3/"	3/1866	4/78	Phaeton	
Hector	0-4-0	4'9"	15x24	F		"		5/76	Goliath	
Milo	2-4-0	5'6"	15x20	S	575	"	3/1863	6/78	Phaeton	
Sunbeam	2-2-2	"	"	"	578	4/"	6/1865 2-4-0	12/73	Aurora	
Phantom	"	"	"	"	579	"	2/1863 2-4-0	4/76	"	
Hurricane	0-4-0	4'9"	15x24	F		5/"		5/69	Goliath	
Fire King	2-4-0	5'6"	15x20	W		7/1849	12/1870	9/82	Phaeton	
Thunderer	0-4-0	4'9"	15x24	F		"		5/76	Goliath	
Vampire	2-4-0	5'6"	15x20	W		"	7/1867	7/72	Phaeton	
Phoenix	0-6-0	4'9"	18x24	FP		12/"	12/1869 16"cyls.	9/80	Iron Duke	

No.	Name	Type	Wheels	Cyls	Makers	Works No	Built	Rebuilt	W'drawn	Class
44	JOHN BULL	2·4·0	5'0"	16×20	W		"	$^{12}/_{1864}$ 2·4·0T	$^9/_{80}$	John Bull
45	CALIBAN	"	"	"	"		$^1/_{1850}$	$^1/_{1865}$ 2·4·0T	$^9/_{80}$	"
46	IRON DUKE	0·6·0	4'9"	18×24	S	639	"	$^1/_{1870}$ 16"cyls.	$^9/_{80}$	Iron Duke
47	PLUTO	0·4·2	4'9"	15×22	"	642	$^3/$ "	$^4/_{1857}$	$^5/_{76}$	Pluto
48	CERBERUS	"	"	"	"	643	"		$^{12}/_{70}$	"
49	GAZELLE	2·2·2	5'6"	15×20	W	$^4/$ "	$^2/_{1868}$ 2·4·0 $^7/_{1875}$	$^9/_{80}$	Venus
50	BANSHEE	"	"	"	"		"	$^6/_{1868}$ 2·4·0	$^{10}/_{73}$	"
51	CENTAUR	2·4·0	5'0"	16×20	S	651	"		$^6/_{76}$	John Bull
52	GORGON	"	"	"	"	652	$^5/$ "		$^5/_{76}$	"
53	VIVID	2·2·2	5'6"	15×20	W		$^{10}/$ "	1870 2·4·0	$^6/_{80}$	Venus
54	REINDEER	"	"	"	"		$^{11}/$ "	$^4/_{1873}$ 2·4·0	$^{10}/_{80}$	"
55	ROSSENDALE	0·6·0	4'9"	16×24	"		$^{11}/_{1852}$	$^3/_{1873}$	$^8/_{82}$	Rossendale
56	AGAMEMNON	"	"	"	"		$^1/_{1853}$	$^1/_{1868}$	$^7/_{81}$	"
57	HANNIBAL	"	"	"	"		$^7/$ "	$^{10}/_{1874}$	$^9/_{82}$	"
58	DUGDALE	"	"	"	"		$^3/_{1854}$	$^2/_{1870}$	$^7/_{81}$	"
59	ULYSSES	"	"	"	SS	330	$^7/_{1856}$	$^6/_{1868}$	$^6/_{76}$	Ulysses
60	SPHINX	"	"	"	"	329	"	$^7/_{1874}$	$^9/_{82}$	"
61	NESTOR	"	"	"	"	331	$^8/$ "		$^8/_{81}$	"
62	MEMNON	"	"	"	"	332	"		$^5/_{77}$	"
63	SESOSTRIS	"	"	"	"	333	"		$^2/_{80}$	"
64	CHARON	0·6·0	4'10"	15×24	MP	95	$^7/_{1857}$	$^7/_{1871}$	$^7/_{81}$	Charon
65	GIRAFFE	2·4·0	6'0"	16×20	BP	70	"	1869	$^{11}/_{78}$	Giraffe To L.Y.R. 8
66	ANTELOPE	"	"	"	"	71	"	1869	$^8/_{79}$	" " 8
67	MACEDON	0·6·0	4'10"	15×24	MP	110	$^5/_{1859}$	$^{12}/_{1874}$	$^7/_{81}$	Charon
73	BLACKLOCK	2·4·0	5'6"	16×20	ELR		$^3/_{1862}$	$^3/_{1871}$	$^{11}/_{82}$	Craven
80	CRAVEN	"	"	16×22	"		$^9/_{1863}$	$^3/_{1877}$	$^{11}/_{92}$	"
1	ODIN	2·4·0T	5'6"	16×22	"		$^1/_{1867}$	1868 TENDER	$^7/_{82}$	Clio. } As rebuilt
3	CLIO	"	"	"	"		"	1869 TENDER	$^8/_{82}$	" } included i
18	TITAN	"	"	"	"		$^9/$ "	1869 TENDER	$^{11}/_{82}$	" } Craven Cl
113	JUNO	2·4·0	"	"	"		$^{10}/_{1871}$		$^2/_{86}$	Juno
16	PEGASUS	"	"	"	"		$^1/_{1872}$		$^2/_{86}$	Craven
146	THOR	"	"	"	"		$^1/_{1876}$		$^2/_{01}$	"
638	PHANTOM	"	"	"	"		$^4/$ "		$^{10}/_{92}$	"
608	JUPITER	2·4·0	5'6"	16×22	ELR		$^5/_{1876}$		$^5/_{93}$	Craven
651	CENTAUR	"	"	"	"		$^6/$ "		$^8/_{92}$	"
662	—	"	"	16×24	"		$^5/_{1877}$		$^2/_{98}$	"

MAKERS —

BP	BEYER, PEACOCK & CO., MANCHESTER.	HF	HAIGH FOUNDRY. WIGAN.
ELR	EAST LANCASHIRE RLY. BURY WORKS.	MP	LANCASHIRE & YORKSHIRE RLY.
F	WM. FAIRBAIRN & SONS. MANCHESTER.	S	SHARP BROS. MANCHESTER.
FC	FENTON & CRAVEN, LEEDS.	SS	STOTHERT & SLAUGHTER. BRISTOL.
FP	FAWCETT, PRESTON & CO. LIVERPOOL.	W	RICHARD WALKER & BROTHER, BURY

LOCOMOTIVE DIMENSIONS.

CLASS	NUMBERS	DATE	MAKERS	TYPE	WHEELS	CYLS.	BOILER DIAM.	BOILER LENGTH	BOILER C/L	BOILER PRESS.	BOILER TUBES	HEATING SURFACE TUBES	HEATING SURFACE F'BOX	HEATING SURFACE TOTAL	GRATE AREA	WHEEL BASE	TOTAL	TRACTIVE EFFORT	
MEDUSA	1. 3. 10. 18.	1846	WALKER	2-2-2	3'6". 5'0". 3'6"	13"x18"	3'7"	9'6"	6'0"	110	147x1¾"	533	70	603	10·7	5'9"+6'11"	12'8"	4740	1. REBUILT AS 2-4-0T (POSSIBLY ALL FOUR)
ROACH	2. 4. 5. 6.	1846	FENTON	2-2-2	3'7". 5'6". 3'7"	°15"x20"	3'9"	13'0"	6'1"	120	142x2"	980·5	62	1042·5	15·0	6'0"+5'9"	11'9"	6954	
"	REBUILT	1848	"	2-4-0	" " "	"	3'9"	10'0"	6'1"	"	"	754·2	62	816·2	15·0	6'0"+7'0"	13'0"	6954	
"	REBUILT	1858	"	0-6-0	4'9"	15"x20"	"	"	"	"	"	"	"	"	"	"	"	8052	
BACCHUS	7. 8. 9. 11.	1846	SHARP	2-2-2	3'6". 5'0". 3'6"	15"x20"	3'9"	10'1"	6'0"	"	147x1¾"	690·3	57·9	748·2	12·2	7'3"+7'3"	14'6"	7650	
SAMSON	12. 19. 20. 22. 13.	1847	HAIGH	0-6-0	4'9"	15"x24"	3'9"	13'0"	6'2"	"	142x2"	980·5	62	1042·5	15·0	6'0"+5'9"	11'9"	9663	
AURORA	14. 15. 21. 37. 38	"	SHARP	2-2-2	3'6". 5'6". 3'6"	15"x20"	3'9"	10'0"	6'0"	"	147x1¾"	690·3	57·9	748·2	12·2	5'8"+7'0"	12'8"	6954	
PEGASUS	16. 17.	"	HAWTHORN	0-4-2	5'0". 3'6"	15"x21"	3'10"	10'0"	6'4"	"	106x2"	650	55	705	11·0	7'3"+6'6"	13'9"	8062	
"	REBUILT	1863	"	2-4-0	3'6". 5'6"	15"x20"	4'0"	10'0"	6'2"	140	170x1¾"	905·5	69·5	975	14·9	6'0"+7'3"	13'3"	8113	
ELK	23	1848	HAIGH	2-2-2															NO DETAILS KNOWN
GOLIATH	24. 32. 35. 39. 41.	"	FAIRBAIRN	0-4-0	4'9"	15"x24"	3'10"	10'6"	6'0"	120	146x2"	805	45	850	12·0	8'7"	8'7"	9663	
VENUS	25. 26. 27. 28. 29. 31. 49. 50. 53. 54	"	WALKER	2-2-2	3'9". 5'6". 3'9"	15"x20"	4'0"	10'0"	6'1"	"	147x1¾"	690·3	57·9	748·2	11·7	6'3"+7'6"	13'9"	6954	
JOHN BULL	44. 45. 51. 52.	1849	"	2-4-0	3'9". 5'0".	16"x20"	"	"	"	"	170x1¾"	905·5	69·5	975	14·7	6'3"+8'6"	14'9"	8704	44, 45 REBUILT AS 2-4-0T
PHAETON	30. 33. 34. 36. 40. 42.	"	{SHARP / WALKER}	"	3'9". 5'6".	15"x20"	3'10"	10'0"	6'1"	"	"	"	"	"	"	"	"	6955	
IRON DUKE	43. 46.	1850	FAWCETT PRESTON SHARP	0-6-0	4'9"	18"x24"	3'9"	14'1"	6'1"	"	133x2"	1041	107	1148	12·6	6'11"+5'3"	12'2"	13914	CYLS. REDUCED TO 16"x24"
PLUTO	47. 48.	"	SHARP	0-4-2	4'9". 3'6".	15"x22"	3'9"	10'4"	6'0"	"	145x2"	800	66	866	12·0	7'0"+7'0"	14'0"	8857	
ROSSENDALE	55. 56. 57. 58	1852	WALKER	0-6-0	4'9"	16"x24"	3'9"	13'0"	6'2"	"	142x2"	981	63	1044	15·0	7'7"+5'0"	12'7"	9663	
ULYSSES	59. 60. 61. 62. 63.	1856	SLAUGHTER	0-6-0	4'9"	16"x24"	3'9"	10'0"	6'5"	130	143x1¾"	693	87	780	15·1	6'0"+7'4"	13'4"	11910	
GIRAFFE	65. 66.	1857	BEYER PEACOCK	2-4-0	3'6". 6'0"	°16"x20"	3'6"	10'4½"	5'10"	"	371x1⅜" x5'5" long	628	66(c) 120	814	16·1	6'5½"+8'3"	14'8½"	7857	(c) COMBUSTION CHAMBER
CHARON	64. 67	1857	L.Y.R.	0-6-0	4'10"	15"x24"	3'9"	10'1½"	6'3"	"	140x2⅛"	809	86	895	14·4	7'3"+7'3"	14'6"	10287	
CRAVEN	8. 16. 38. 51. 62. 73. 80. 146	1862	E.L.R.	2-4-0	3'9". 5'6"	16"x22"	4'0"	10'0"	6'3"	140	170x1¾"	905·5	69·5	975	14·9	6'4"+8'5"	14'9"	10155	
CLIO	1. 3. 18	1867	E.L.R.	2-4-0T	3'9". 5'6"	16"x24"	4'0"	10'0"	6'3"	"	"	"	"	"	"	7'3"+8'0"	15'3"	11077	
JUNO	113	1871	E.L.R.	2-4-0	3'9". 5'6"	16"x22"	4'0"	9'7"	6'1"	"	177x1¾"	780	60	840	11·5	5'9"+6'11"	12'8"	10155	

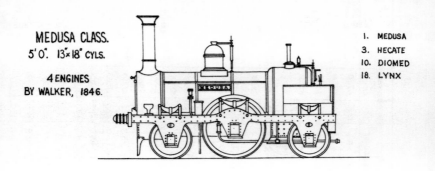

MEDUSA CLASS.
5' 0". 13"×18" CYLS.

4 ENGINES
BY WALKER, 1846.

1. MEDUSA
3. HECATE
10. DIOMED
18. LYNX

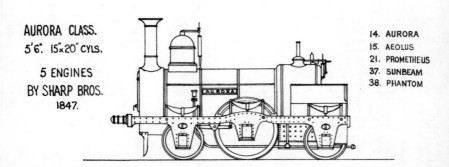

AURORA CLASS.
5' 6". 15"×20" CYLS.

5 ENGINES
BY SHARP BROS.
1847.

14. AURORA
15. AEOLUS
21. PROMETHEUS
37. SUNBEAM
38. PHANTOM

ROACH CLASS.
AS BUILT.

4 ENGINES BY
FENTON & CRAVEN
1846.

5' 6". 15"×20" CYLS.

2. ROACH
4. SPITFIRE
5. CYCLOPS
6. SALAMANDER

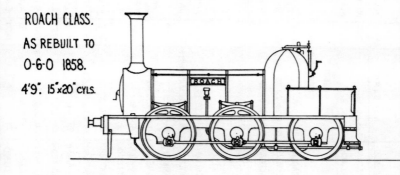

ROACH CLASS.
AS REBUILT TO
0-6-0 1858.

4' 9". 15"×20" CYLS.

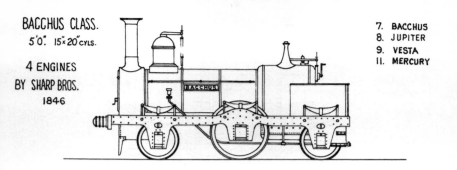

BACCHUS CLASS.
5'0". 15"×20"CYLS.

4 ENGINES
BY SHARP BROS.
1846

7. BACCHUS
8. JUPITER
9. VESTA
11. MERCURY

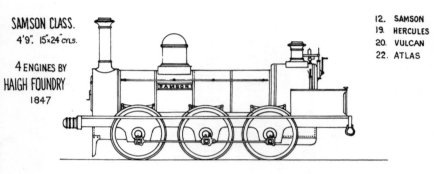

SAMSON CLASS.
4'9". 15"×24"CYLS.

4 ENGINES BY
HAIGH FOUNDRY
1847

12. SAMSON
19. HERCULES
20. VULCAN
22. ATLAS

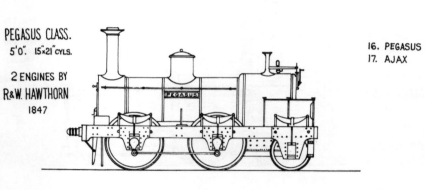

PEGASUS CLASS.
5'0". 15"×21"CYLS.

2 ENGINES BY
R.&W. HAWTHORN
1847

16. PEGASUS
17. AJAX

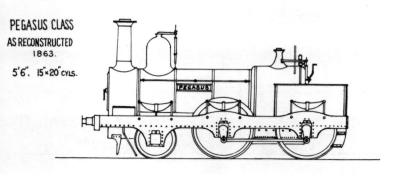

PEGASUS CLASS
AS RECONSTRUCTED
1863.

5'6". 15"×20"CYLS.

GOLIATH CLASS.

4'9". 15"×24" CYLS.

5 ENGINES BY
FAIRBAIRN & Cº
1848

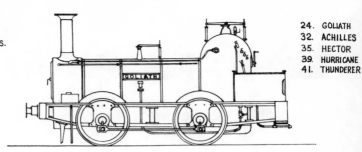

24.	GOLIATH
32.	ACHILLES
35.	HECTOR
39.	HURRICANE
41.	THUNDERER

VENUS CLASS.

5'6". 15"×20" CYLS.

10 ENGINES

BY WALKER.
1848-1850

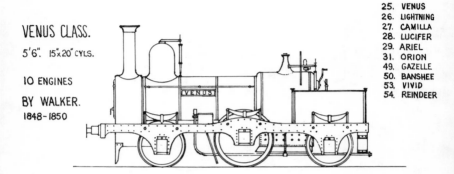

25.	VENUS
26.	LIGHTNING
27.	CAMILLA
28.	LUCIFER
29.	ARIEL
31.	ORION
49.	GAZELLE
50.	BANSHEE
53.	VIVID
54.	REINDEER

PHAETON CLASS.

5'6". 15"×20" CYLS.

2 ENGINES BY
SHARP BROS.,
4 ENGINES BY
WALKER
1849

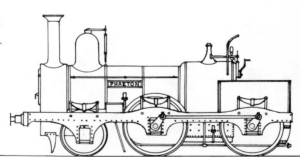

30.	PHAETON
33.	MAZEPPA
40.	FIRE KING
42.	VAMPIRE
	(WALKER)

34.	TAMERLANE
36.	MILO
	(SHARP)

| 44. | JOHN BULL |
| 45. | CALIBAN |

JOHN BULL CLASS.

AS REBUILT 1863/4.
5'0" 16"×20" CYLS.

2 ENGINES
BY WALKER
1849

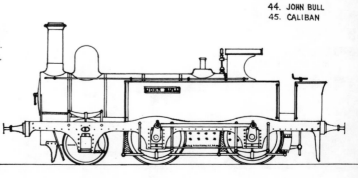

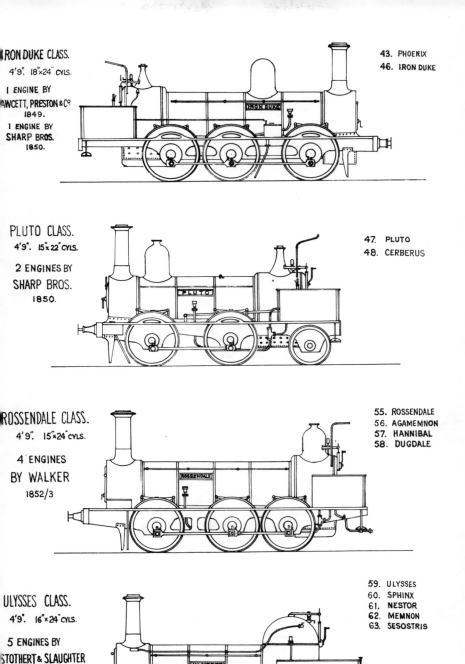

IRON DUKE CLASS.
4'9". 18"×24" CYLS.

1 ENGINE BY
FAWCETT, PRESTON & C⁰
1849.

1 ENGINE BY
SHARP BROS.
1850.

43. PHOENIX
46. IRON DUKE

PLUTO CLASS.
4'9". 15"×22" CYLS.

2 ENGINES BY
SHARP BROS.
1850.

47. PLUTO
48. CERBERUS

ROSSENDALE CLASS.
4'9". 15"×24" CYLS.

4 ENGINES
BY WALKER
1852/3

55. ROSSENDALE
56. AGAMEMNON
57. HANNIBAL
58. DUGDALE

ULYSSES CLASS.
4'9". 16"×24" CYLS.

5 ENGINES BY
STOTHERT & SLAUGHTER
1856.

59. ULYSSES
60. SPHINX
61. NESTOR
62. MEMNON
63. SESOSTRIS

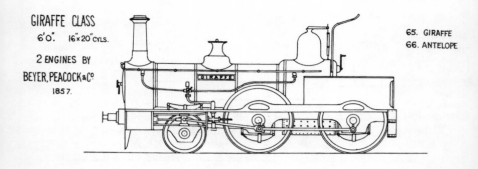

GIRAFFE CLASS
6'0". 16"×20"CYLS.

2 ENGINES BY
BEYER, PEACOCK & Cº
1857.

65. GIRAFFE
66. ANTELOPE

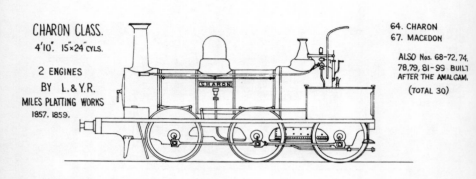

CHARON CLASS.
4'10". 15"×24"CYLS.

2 ENGINES
BY L.&Y.R.
MILES PLATTING WORKS
1857. 1859.

64. CHARON
67. MACEDON

ALSO Nos. 68-72, 74,
78, 79, 81-99 BUILT
AFTER THE AMALGAM.
(TOTAL 30)

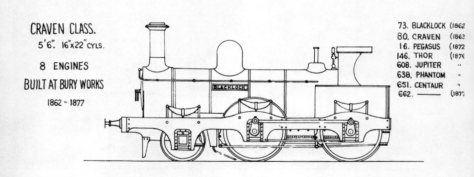

CRAVEN CLASS.
5'6". 16"×22"CYLS.

8 ENGINES
BUILT AT BURY WORKS
1862 ~ 1877

73. BLACKLOCK (1862
80. CRAVEN (1863
16. PEGASUS (1872
146. THOR (1876
608. JUPITER "
638. PHANTOM "
651. CENTAUR "
662. ——— (1877

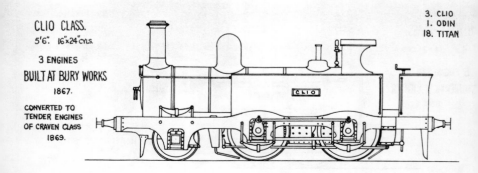

CLIO CLASS.
5'6". 16"×24"CYLS.

3 ENGINES
BUILT AT BURY WORKS
1867.

CONVERTED TO
TENDER ENGINES
OF CRAVEN CLASS
1869.

3. CLIO
1. ODIN
18. TITAN

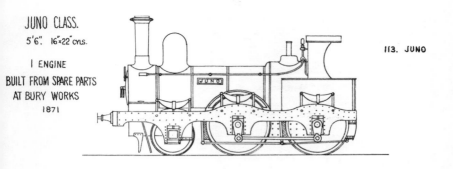

JUNO CLASS.

5'6". 16"x22" cyls.

I ENGINE
BUILT FROM SPARE PARTS
AT BURY WORKS
1871

113. JUNO

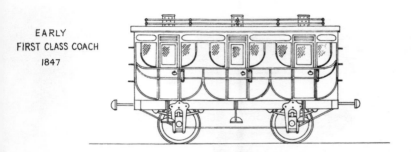

EARLY
FIRST CLASS COACH
1847

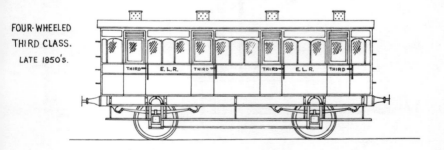

FOUR-WHEELED
THIRD CLASS.
LATE 1850's.

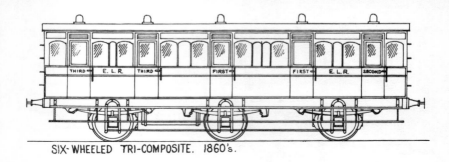

SIX-WHEELED TRI-COMPOSITE. 1860's.

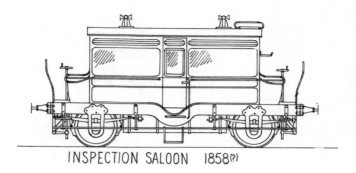

INSPECTION SALOON 1858(?)

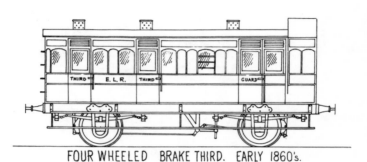

FOUR WHEELED BRAKE THIRD. EARLY 1860's.

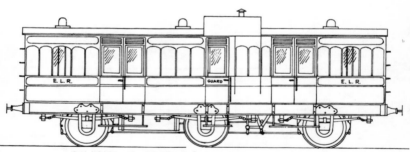

SIX-WHEELED BRAKE & PARCELS VAN. 1860's.

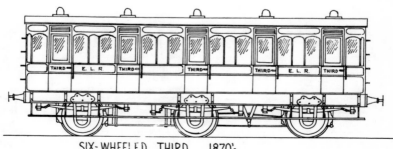

SIX-WHEELED THIRD. 1870's

CHAPTER 10
Engine Sheds

There were not many sheds for locomotives on the E.L.R. system, and some of them seem to be shrouded in mystery. However, from the researches of Mr. A. Barlow, a few notes can be made of them.

Accrington
The first shed here was opened in 1848, and was situated in the middle of the triangular junction. It had two through roads, and held six engines. The situation was very cramped, and allowed no room for expansion, though space was found for a coal stack and turntable. By 1857 there were frenzied letters going to the directors from the shed foreman complaining of the completely inadequate facilities, as twelve engines were stationed there, and of the inability of the fitters to work in the shed owing to the thick smoke. Nothing was done, and by 1869 the foreman requested permission to use an old building some little distance away on the Blackburn side, as he had then 22 engines with space for only six. Plans for a new shed by the side of the Blackburn line were drawn up in 1871, and after some squabbling with contractors, this shed, with accommodation for 24 engines, was opened in 1873. This was still not the end, for in 1899 a third shed was built some 300 yards further westwards, and the 1873 shed turned over to carriages. This final shed, a dead-end building, with a capacity of 48 engines, remained in use until 1970, when it was demolished.

Blackburn
A shed was opened here in 1846 by the Blackburn & Preston Railway, with a single road for two engines, and adjoining the Bolton Road goods yard. In 1848 it was decided to extend the shed by using the materials from the shed at Farington, and this was carried out. This points to the assumption that both sheds were built of wood. It was again extended in 1863, to a capacity of 16 engines, but was closed and demolished in 1881, when the new brick-built shed at Lower Darwen was opened. Part of the site was utilised to extend the goods yard.
There was a second shed at Blackburn, erected by the B.D.&B.R. in 1847, adjoining its own station in Bolton Road. It had two through roads, for six engines, and was entered from the Darwen direction. When the company was taken over jointly by the E.L.R. and L.&Y.R. in 1855, this shed was closed and demolished.

Bootle
The original shed here was put up in 1848, and was designed to hold twelve engines, six for each company (E.L.R. and L.&Y.R.). It was a

long, narrow shed with two through roads, and access to the main line at both ends. It was situated where later the Southport line joined the main route (Sandhills), and had to be removed when that line was built in 1851. Thenceforward the L.&Y.R. engines were removed to a new shed at Sandhills, and the E.L.R. engines reverted to Tithebarn Street.

Liverpool

Tithebarn Street had two sheds, one for each company, opened in 1849. The E.L.R. shed was built of brick, and was of the dead-end type, with a turntable. Its exact location is doubtful, as it fell victim to the massive earthworks entailed for the new Great Howard Street goods yard in 1876. When anything untoward happened at this shed, the engines were diverted to Sandhills.

Bury

Built by the M.B.&R.R. in 1846, this shed was known as Buckley Wells, from the district of Bury in which it was situated, about ¼ mile south of the station, and was adjacent to the works. It was decided in 1848 that the shed needed to be enlarged, and another section was added. Nothing more was done until the shed was closed on 1 January 1876, the old shed then becoming an erecting shop for the works. After much argument about sites and costs, the new shed was built, of the dead-end type, with eight roads. In 1921 it had an allocation of 61 engines. It was closed on 12 April 1965.

Ormskirk

Perring, the engineer of the E.L.R., reported in 1853 that it was imperative to have a shed here for the working of the Skelmersdale branch. He suggested that a wooden building being used as a temporary workshop at Bury could be utilised for this purpose, but this had still not been resolved in 1856. It was partially settled by the amalgamation in 1859, when the E.L.R. could then use the joint L.&Y.R./St. Helens Railway shed. This, however, was totally inadequate. At some date prior to 1873 the shed was badly damaged by fire, and a temporary shed was requested. As usual, decisions were shelved, and in 1883 another request for a shed to hold twelve engines was put in. With typical L.&Y.R. procrastination, this shed was actually built in 1893, and was closed on 29 September 1935.

Preston

At Farington the Blackburn & Preston Railway erected a small wooden shed to hold two engines, in the fork of the junction. It seems to have fallen into disuse very early, as it was found easier to use the shed of the Preston & Lancaster Railway, to the north of Preston station. This was used by E.L.R. and L.&Y.R. engines until 1881, when Lostock Hall shed was built. The Farington shed was transported to Blackburn to extend the shed there in 1848. From the opening of the new Butler Street extension of Preston station in 1850, a small shed there was used by E.L.R. engines; this shed became disused on the opening of Lostock Hall, and its site used to extend the goods yard.

Ramsbottom
A small wooden shed was erected by the E.L.R. in 1846, to hold one engine used for banking duties up to Baxenden summit. By 1870 it was in use for goods purposes; the exact date when it ceased to be an engine shed is not known.

Salford
The situation at Salford is complicated, and the history conflicting. The L.&Y.R. had a shed in Oldfield Road, which had been erected by the Manchester & Bolton Railway in 1838. For a time the E.L.R. used it as well, but the situation becoming increasingly cramped, and with the bad blood existing between the E.L.R. and L.&Y.R., the former company suggested a shed of their own, but land was at a premium. The E.L.R. proposed an extra platform at Oldfield Road station and an engine shed, in 1854, and a piece of land owned by the two companies was allocated, but the E.L.R. did not consider this a suitable site, and preferred one at Pendleton. As usual, nothing was done, and the subject came up again in the following year. At last something was settled, and the E.L.R. built a shed in Hope Street (on the opposite side of Oldfield Road) in 1856, with three dead-end roads and a capacity of twelve engines. In 1860 there was a complaint about the shed being in disrepair, but nothing was done. Two years later the shed had deteriorated so badly that something had to be done, but "only where absolutely necessary, and as cheaply as possible". In 1864 an estimate was produced for an entirely new shed, but the cost of the land was deemed prohibitive. Whatever was proposed at Salford, there was some snag or other. Every succeeding year saw new proposals, reports, etc., all to no purpose, until at last in 1871 Hope Street shed was torn down and completely rebuilt with eight dead-end roads. With this rebuilding, the old 1838 shed was demolished, and its engines transferred to the new shed. It was in an awkward situation, and not ideal for any of the services required of it, but it continued in use until Agecroft shed was opened in 1889, when Salford ceased to have an engine shed.

Southport
Southport's earliest shed was erected by the Liverpool, Crosby & Southport Railway in 1848, and consisted of nothing more than a roof supported on poles. In 1853, the sides were boarded in, to provide some sort of protection from wind-blown sand. In 1855 the L.&Y.R. took over the L.C.&S.R., and on the joint line from Wigan being opened, the L.&Y.R. began using the original shed. This left no room for the E.L.R.,

so they built a shed of their own, to hold four engines, in the coal yard off London Street. Some alterations were made to Chapel Street station in 1861, and the old L.C.&S.R. shed was obstructing the work, but it was impossible to send the engines to the E.L.R. shed, since there was no room for them. The foreman pointed out the position to the locomotive committee, who thereupon rescinded the order to pull down the old shed. Since the station alterations could not be completed, trains suffered long delays in having to wait for other trains to clear the platforms, and this went on until 1870, when the E.L.R. shed was enlarged to hold eight engines. In 1883 further alterations were made to Chapel Street station which solved several problems, but it was not unti 1885 that the old L.C.&S. shed was removed. March 1890 saw the opening of a large new shed on the site of the E.L.R. one. This shed held 40 engines, and remained in continuous use until finally closed in May 1966.

Printed by Bookmag, Henderson Road, Inverness